IPS

Beyond the "Vietnam Syndrome"

U.S. Interventionism in the 1980s

Michael T. Klare

The Institute for Policy Studies is a non-partisan research institute. The views expressed in this study are solely those of the author.

Each chapter of *Beyond the 'Vietnam Syndrome'* is a revised and updated version of an article which first appeared in one of several publications. In each case, such usage of the original text was done with the permission of the publisher. The original titles and copyright data follow:

Chapter I originally appeared as: "Curing the Vietnam Syndrome," *The Nation* (October 13, 1979); copyright 1979 by Michael T. Klare.

Chapter II originally appeared as: "The Brown Doctrine: Have R.D.F., Will Travel," *The Nation* (March 8, 1980); copyright 1980 by Michael T. Klare.

Chapter III originally appeared as: "Is Exxon Worth Dying For?," *The Progressive* (July, 1980); copyright 1980 by The Progressive, Inc.; extracts used with permission.

Chapter IV originally appeared as: "Resource Wars," *Harper's* (January, 1981); copyright 1980 by Harper's Magazine; all rights reserved; extracts reprinted from the January 1981 issue by special permission.

Chapter V originally appeared as: "An Army in Search of a War," *The Progressive* (February, 1981); copyright 1981 by The Progressive, Inc.; extracts used with permission.

Chapter VI originally appeared as: "The New Counterinsurgency," *The Nation* (March 14, 1981); copyright 1981 by Michael T. Klare.

The Appendix originally appeared as: "The 'Power Projection' Gap," *The Nation* (June 9, 1979); copyright 1979 by Michael T. Klare.

All revisions and all other contents copyright 1981 by Michael T. Klare and the Institute for Policy Studies.

Published by the Institute for Policy Studies

Copies of this book are available from the Institute for Policy Studies, 1901 Q Street, N.W., Washington, D.C. 20009 or the Transnational Institute, Paulus Potterstraat 20, 1071 DA, Amsterdam, The Netherlands.

First Printing: 1981

ISBN 0-89758-027-3

85300

ABOUT THE AUTHOR

MICHAEL T. KLARE is a Fellow of the Institute for Policy Studies and Director of its Militarism and Disarmament Project. Formerly a Visiting Fellow at Princeton University's Center of International Studies and a Research Director for the North American Congress on Latin America (NACLA), he is author of *War Without End: American Planning for the Next Vietnams* (Knopf, 1972), and a forthcoming book on the international arms trade. Dr. Klare writes regularly on international affairs for *The Nation, Harper's, The Progressive, Bulletin of the Atomic Scientists*, and *Le Monde Diplomatique*. He hold degrees from Columbia University and the Union Graduate School.

TABLE OF CONTENTS

FOREWORD

MICHAEL KLARE'S essays make important reading in the
Reagan years. He traces the evolution of the so-called
Vietnam Syndrome and shows how the official attitudes in
Washington have veered once more in the direction of
armed intervention. The Reagan answer to the Vietnam
Syndrome is a replay of the Cold War of John Foster Dulles.
The rhetoric of the 1980s now bears a remarkable similarity
to that of the 1950s. The impulse to recreate Mr. Dulles' *Pax
Americana*, when the United States held sway in the world
with a maximum use of threat and minimum use of force, has
proven irresistible. However, the world of the 1980s is not
the world of the 1950s. The possibility of organizing that
part of the world not controlled or dominated by the Soviet
Union around the ideology of "anti-communism" no longer
exists. Not only has the so-called "Communist bloc" ceased
to be that for more than a generation, but it is evident that
profound evolution is taking place within the Soviet orbit
itself, notably in Poland. At a time when Soviet models and
Soviet ideology seem to have lost much of their appeal, there
are few nations in the world that can be galvanized by the
prospect of an anti-communist crusade. This is now
especially clear in Europe, where the necessity of co-
existence and detente are so obvious. The more the Administration seeks to line America's allies up to carry on a global
Cold War, the more neutralism in Europe is likely to grow.
Detente was far more than a political slogan. It was an
historical era, the consequences of which can be neither
ignored nor eliminated. The Soviet Union and the worldwide fight against communism has always served as the
justification for interventions in strategic areas of the Third
World which have been undertaken by the United States for
other reasons. The Reagan Administration began by identi-
fying El Salvador as the "test case" for proving a number of
its favorite theses about the world: first, that the Soviet
Union and Cuba were behind national independence
struggles; two, that the judicious use or threat of military
power could, liberal critics to the contrary, produce favor-   vii

able political changes in the world; and three, that the United States has the power to force allies and neutrals to support its policies of intervention, no matter how distasteful they may find them. All three assumptions are wrong. For this reason the Administration, despite its tough talk, appears to be floundering in its foreign policy.

The Administration came to office promising to restore America to what Dean Acheson once called "situations of strength." Obviously, more than a military buildup was required. The Government would have to learn once again to speak with one voice on foreign policy issues. It would have to demonstrate strong public support for its program to restore American power. It would have to strengthen America's ties with its major allies. Most important, it would have to demonstrate that the nation's economy was vital enough to sustain our global commitments.

So far, the Administration has succeeded in confusing friend and foe alike. According to Secretary of State Alexander M. Haig, Jr., the Russians are powerful enough to orchestrate much of the world's mischief, yet he says they are about to fall into the very ashcan of history that they have been preparing for us. The President's closest advisor, Edwin Meese 3d, announces that military action against Cuba is being considered, but the grain embargo against the Soviet Union is precipitously lifted without even advance notification to our allies.

El Salvador is selected as the critical site to make a stand against the newly discovered worldwide Communist-terrorist conspiracy. But neither the Congress, the Roman Catholic hierarchy, nor our European allies believe that the bloody civil war in that country was invented in Moscow. International terrorism is a fashionable construct to make chaotic and unmanageable events in a dizzying variety of places fit a ready-made strategy for addressing them—much like the "arc of crisis" rhetoric in the Carter Administration—but the Central Intelligence Agency says it has been unable to confirm the basic facts on which the Administration's paranoid worldview rests. Administration spokesmen claim that America would lose prestige if El Salvador's "moderately repressive" torturers and murderers, whom we are generously supplying with helicopters and rifles, should fall.

Thus, the Administration is setting that country up to be

the new Vietnam. Whether a single additional adviser or even one infantry platoon is ever sent there, the Administration has already invested so much in that operation that this nation cannot help emerging from the involvement weaker, not stronger. Having announced that a political solution that includes the left is a major defeat, we have once again advertised our impotence. Having made support of our El Salvador policy a loyalty test for our allies in Europe and watched them flunk, the Administration has strengthened neutralist sentiment on the Continent and given a boost to the antiwar movement in both America and Europe.

Earlier administrations justified armed interventions and covert operations on ideological grounds. The United States was promoting freedom. It was fighting the "good fight against communism," to use the words of Allen Dulles. Today there is far more emphasis on the short-term strategic interests of the United States, principally with respect to oil and vital minerals. Michael Klare points out how the minerals and petroleum issues have been used and misused to justify new strategies of intervention. There is perhaps no better illustration of the distortion of American priorities. For a fraction of what is projected to be spent in new ships, planes, rapid deployment forces, and new generations of weapons the United States could significantly reduce its dependency on foreign oil. Dependency on strategic minerals, despite much alarmist talk, is by no means so serious. But even here great gains could be made in improving American national security by investing in research and alternative exploration. While it is true that certain minerals are derived from a very few strategic sources and that they are indispensible for certain products—notably chrome, manganese, and gold—much of what they are used for—stainless steel salad forks, gold-plated lipsticks, etc.—are not exactly crucial to national survival. Indeed there is no reason to believe that the United States cannot have all the salad forks the American people want without threatening to blow up or shoot up other countries. Few nations have much interest in withholding vital minerals from the biggest single market in the world. But it is some indication of how distorted our thinking as a nation is that we now hear so much loose talk about the need to use force and to risk war for supposedly "vital interests." The only truly vital interest of the American people is peace. It is the task of diplomacy to figure out how peace can be preserved without sacrificing either the freedom or the economic health of the American people. One thing is sure. A holy war against national liberation movements around the world that need not be our enemies can secure neither.

—Richard J. Barnet
Washington, D.C.
August 1981

ACKNOWLEDGMENTS

The writing of *Beyond the 'Vietnam Syndrome'* was a natural outgrowth of my work as Director of the Militarism and Disarmament Project of the Institute for Policy Studies, and thus could not have been completed without the assistance and support of all my colleagues at IPS. I am particularly indebted to Daniel Volman, Cynthia Arnson, and Steven Daggett of the Militarism & Disarmament Staff for their help in research and their constructive criticism of my analysis, and especially to Delia Miller for her multiple contributions at every stage in the preparation of the book. Thanks are also due to all those at IPS whose assistance, criticism, and support has been so unstinting over the years, and especially to Bob Borosage, Richard Barnet, Marcus Raskin, Saul Landau, Fred Halliday, Eqbal Ahmad, Alyce Wiley, and Anne McWilliams.

While the views and opinions expressed in *Beyond the 'Vietnam Syndrome'* are wholly my own, my analysis of U.S. policy developed through a process of continuous inter-action with other researchers and analysts, many of whom provided valuable insights and encouragement. In this regard, I owe particular gratitude to: Max Holland and Bill Goodfellow of the Center for International Policy, David Johnson of the Center for Defense Information, Victor Navasky of *The Nation*, Erwin Knoll of *The Progressive*, Matthew Stevenson of *Harper's*, Prof. Alan Wolfe of Queens College, Prof. Richard Falk of Princeton University, Daniel Ellsberg, and William Arkin. And because I developed many of the themes of this book while speaking at teach-ins, conferences, and lecture series, I wish to thank all of the fine people in the United States, Canada, Mexico, Europe, and Australia who have invited me to speak in their communities and who asked those tough questions which forced me to rethink and refine my ideas. Greetings to you all!

—Michael T. Klare
Washington, D.C., June 1981

I.
THE ASSAULT ON THE "VIETNAM SYNDROME"

For seven years, the United States fought a costly and ultimately futile war in Southeast Asia. When the war in Vietnam ended, a new war began. Not a war with guns and bullets, but a war with words—the war to reverse the "Vietnam Syndrome." Although this propaganda war is still underway, it has already had a decisive impact on American politics and may, when the last battle is finally decided, affect the course of history even more profoundly than the Vietnam conflict itself.[1]

Stated simply, the "Vietnam Syndrome" is the American public's disinclination to engage in further military interventions in internal Third World conflicts. For many Americans, this "Syndrome" is a prudent and beneficial alternative to the interventionist policies which led us into Vietnam in the first place. Not only is it sparing of the lives of our young men and women, but it also facilitates the search for creative, non-military solutions to the problems facing all nations in an increasingly interdependent world. For other Americans, however, the Vietnam Syndrome is an unacceptable restraint on Washington's capability to protect critical U.S. interests abroad. These individuals believe that any reluctance on our part to engage in military action invites attack by hostile forces and thus endangers America's privileged world position. And because they are determined to revive intervention as a legitimate instrument of U.S. foreign policy, they have launched a vigorous and unceasing campaign to "cure" America of the Vietnam Syndrome.

Although, for most of the past ten years, U.S. leaders attempted to steer a middle course between these two conflicting outlooks—eschewing involvement in "peripheral" contests like those in Angola (1976) and Nicaragua (1978) while sanctioning intervention if needed to protect "vital" interests such as Middle Eastern oil—it is now apparent that the anti-Syndrome forces will not rest until they have secured the total victory of their position. When and if that moment arrives—and it could arrive soon—America may find itself embroiled in a new round of conflicts that will make Vietnam look like a minor skirmish. Until then, however, the Syndrome will continue to act as a brake on aggressive U.S. military behavior abroad, and thus advocates of interventionism will continue to make war on all surviving expressions of this deeply-rooted stance.

When first developed, the Vietnam Syndrome had both institutional and subjective manifestations. Institutionally, the Syndrome assumed a number of specific forms: (1) the War Powers Act, and other legislative restrictions on presidential war-making abroad; (2) the abolition of conscription and the establishment of an all-volunteer service; (3) restrictions on covert operations by the CIA and other intelligence agencies; and (4) military alliances with "surrogate gendarmes" like Iran (under the Shah) and Egypt (under Sadat).

These developments had profound consequences for the entire national security establishment. The Armed Services lost nearly half of their uniformed personnel, thus eliminating future openings for thousands of generals, admirals and other top career officers. The Pentagon budget was reduced (in non-inflated, "real" dollars), causing a significant drop in business for the nation's bloated arms industry. The CIA was forced to undergo an unprecedented public probe of its secret operations, and lost many veteran "spooks" through a massive layoff of senior personnel. All told, it was the greatest institutional setback for the warfare state since the demobilization ordered by President Eisenhower after the Korean War.

More serious than these institutional reverses, however, was the subjective response. Once all U.S. troops had been withdrawn from Indochina, the nation breathed a collective sigh of relief and adopted a "never again" stance on the use of U.S. troops to control political changes in the Third World. Summarizing this perspective in 1975, Senator Edward Kennedy declared that "the lesson [of Vietnam] is that we must throw off the cumbersome mantle of world police-man." In the same spirit, Senator Alan Cranston observed, "The United States should be a peaceful world neighbor instead of a militant world meddler."[2] This view prevailed in 1976, when Congress voted to prohibit U.S. military involvement in Angola (under the so-called "Clark Amendment"), and again a year later, when Washington elected to remain on the sidelines during the Ethiopian-Somalia conflict.

President Carter, who was elected when the Vietnam Syndrome was at its peak, generally adhered to the non-interventionist outlook expressed by Senators Kennedy and Cranston in 1975. Although some of his advisers—particularly Zbigniew Brzezinski—advocated a military response to particular crises, Carter vetoed direct U.S. involvement in such conflicts as the Zaire upheavals of 1976 and 1978, the Iranian Revolution, and the Nicaraguan civil war. And, in the one instance where Carter did sanction the use of force—the abortive hostage rescue mission of April 1980—he confined such action to a small-scale commando raid.

As the 1970s drew to a close, however, more and more policymakers viewed this non-interventionist stance as an intolerable constraint on U.S. power at a time of growing challenges to American interests abroad. These leaders—representing powerful segments of the military, intelligence and business communities—argued that America's unwillingness to use force in responding to minor threats abroad would only invite more serious and intractable challenges later. The Vietnam Syndrome, in their view, actually fosters instability because it encourages hostile powers to exploit the emerging gaps in the West's global security system. "Worldwide stability is being eroded through the retrenchment of American policy and power," James R. Schlesinger wrote in *Fortune* after his dismissal as Secretary of Defense in 1976. "This growing instability reflects visible factors such as the deterioration in the military balance, but also, perhaps more immediately, such invisible factors as the *altered psychological stance* of the United States, a nation apparently withdrawing from the burdens of leadership and power."[3] (Emphasis added.)

For these critics, U.S. non-involvement in Angola, Ethiopia, and Iran constituted a sign of American *weakness*, rather than a calculated policy of restraint. "Vietnam caused

3

a loss of confidence in the ability of the U.S. to defend non-Communist regimes in Third World countries against subversion and military takeovers by Moscow's allies," *Business Week* observed in 1979. "This perception of paralysis was confirmed when the U.S. stood by helplessly as Russian-backed insurgents, aided by Cuban troops, took over Angola. And it was enhanced when the Soviet-aligned Ethiopian government crushed separatist movements in Eritrea and the Ogaden."[4]

For advocates of a renewed interventionist posture, the Vietnam Syndrome is not merely a misguided policy approach, but evidence of a far more profound psychological disorder. "Our internal preoccupations and our political divisions of recent years," Schlesinger avowed, underlie the "growing *infirmity* of American policy." Frequently, these critics used words with psycho-sexual overtones: America's allies have lost confidence in "the *firmness* of American policy;" Europeans deplore "the *faltering* of American purpose;" American restraint has "created an image of U.S. *impotence*."[5] (Emphasis added.)

Because Jimmy Carter generally pursued a non-interventionist approach to overseas conflicts, he became the principal target for such charges. As the 1980 election drew closer, he was often castigated for his timidity and vacillation in dealing with foreign crises. "The Administration's response to the multiplying challenges and disorders abroad," conservative columnist George F. Will charged in *Newsweek*, "has been a litany of things it will not do: interventions it will not contemplate, bases it will not seek, weapons it will not build."[6] When Carter declined to defend the Shah of Iran against a popular upheaval in 1978, Senator Howard Baker spoke for many proponents of intervention when he avowed that White House inaction "invite[s] the interpretation that we do not have the will or the resolve to act under any circumstances." And, in an extraordinary 1979 address to the Coalition for a Democratic Majority, Senator Henry Jackson charged that the Administration's placidity in the face of growing Soviet belligerence has "the mark of appeasement."[7]

These attacks culminated in March 1979 with a special issue of *Business Week* on "The Decline of U.S. Power," featuring a dramatic picture of the Statute of Liberty in tears. Arguing that, since Vietnam, the United States "has

4

been buffeted by an unnerving series of shocks that signal an accelerating erosion of power and influence," the magazine's editors called for a revitalized military capacity to protect U.S. interests abroad. Without a more activist foreign policy, they argued, America's favored economic standing may soon vanish. "The policies set in motion during the Vietnam War are now threatening the way of life built since World War II."[8]

The *Business Week* issue was particularly significant because it constitutes a rare public airing of the intense policy debate which has gripped the U.S. power structure ever since Vietnam. This debate actually originated in the elite struggle over the war itself: after Tet and the appearance of a broad-based antiwar movement at home, the elite world split into factions favoring the continuation of the war and others calling for an American withdrawal. After the war, this debate was transformed into a deeper conflict over America's role in the "post-Vietnam" world. Although U.S. leaders were unanimous in their belief that America had to act decisively to shore up its dominion over the non-Communist world, they were divided both in their perceptions of the principal obstacles to this goal, and also in their strategies for attaining it. This division, which lasted until 1979, underlay the rancorous foreign policy debates which buffeted Washington throughout the 1970s.

The "Traders" and the "Prussians"

One side in this debate, composed largely of corporate managers and international bankers, argued that the greatest threats to U.S. hegemony were divisions within the capitalist world and growing economic nationalism on the part of the Third World. To overcome these difficulties, this group—which I have dubbed the "Traders"—called for greater economic collaboration between the major capitalist powers (and especially between the "trilateral" bloc of America, Japan, and Western Europe) along with the co-optation of Third World elites through token concessions on North-South trade issues. The Soviet Union, while meddlesome, was viewed as a secondary threat because of its economic backwardness and preoccupation with unruly clients and satellites (not to mention former satellites like China). To

5

assure stability in turbulent Third World areas, meanwhile, the Traders sponsored the rise of "surrogate gendarmes" like Iran to assume regional peacekeeping responsibilities.

This approach was challenged, however, by another bloc composed of military officers, intelligence operatives, Cold War intellectuals, arms producers, and some domestic capitalists. This group, which I call the "Prussians," argued that the principal threat to U.S. hegemony was uncontrolled political and social "turbulence" in the Third World, coupled with the growing military assertiveness of the Soviet Union. To guarantee continued U.S. access to the mineral and agricultural wealth of the Third World while ensuring the quiescence of Moscow, this bloc called for a more vigorous U.S. "police" presence abroad plus a massive expansion of America's nuclear arsenal.*

For the most part, the participants in this struggle prefer to conduct their battles in seclusion—in corporate board rooms, private clubs, and exclusive Washington restaurants. Because the debate revolves around the basic underpinnings of American power, and because it is simply not possible to expose the inner workings of elite decision-making to public scrutiny (it is not proper, for instance, to tell a Congressional subcommittee that Cuban intervention in Angola is really good for America because it assures stability in Gulf Oil's Cabinda field), this struggle tends to be translated into other terms when conducted in public.

The most common expression of this struggle, of course, is the dispute over the "Soviet threat." Because data on Soviet military strength is subject to the wide range of interpretations, debate over the size and character of Soviet capabilities is often used as a surrogate for the more profound contest over foreign policy. While the Traders argue that Moscow is far too pre-occupied with domestic problems and growing restiveness in Eastern Europe to embark upon any major confrontations with the West, the Prussians insist that Moscow will use its awesome military muscle to dominate key Third World areas—particularly

---

*The concept of the "Traders and Prussians" should be viewed as an analytical tool rather than as precise sociological classifications. While we can distinguish two poles in this often acrimonious debate, and we can associate a few prominent individuals with one or another of these poles, most U.S. leaders normally hovered somewhere in between until international events or career imperatives forced a more conscious shift to one side.[9]

the Middle East—and thus to undermine the Western economies. And while both sides recognize that it is unlikely that Moscow would ever be foolhardy enough to threaten any *really* vital American interests, like Persian Gulf oil (despite all the talk of Soviet intervention in the Middle East, Moscow has been very, very careful to avoid any action that could be interpreted as a threat to Western oil supplies) the Prussians argue that the mere *existence* of large Soviet forces might encourage maverick Third World governments to be more obstinate in their dealings with the West than they would be otherwise.[10]

The debate over military policy has also arisen in discussions of the Vietnam War itself. While most Americans still believe that we were right to pull U.S. troops out of Indochina, many "realist" intellectuals now argue that we would be better off today in the Middle East and elsewhere if we'd stuck it out in Vietnam and demonstrated our "resolve" to protect vital U.S. interests. (Indeed, Ronald Reagan went so far as to call the Vietnam War "a noble cause" during the 1980 presidential campaign.[11])

As these debates proceeded, both sides demonstrated assorted strengths and weaknesses. By choosing early to support Jimmy Carter in 1976, the Traders succeeded in placing some of their leading representatives in high Administration posts. Cyrus Vance became Secretary of State, Paul Warnke was named director of the Arms Control & Disarmament Agency, and Andrew Young was made U.S. Ambassador to the United Nations. The Prussians, on the other hand, proved adept at manipulating public opinion and at using the "Soviet threat" anxiety to mobilize opposition to Administration policies. For a time, Paul Nitze's "Committee on the Present Danger" and other Prussian organizations were being quoted as regularly as the White House itself.

While the two sides in this debate once appeared evenly matched, by the late 1970s the Trader position began to exhibit major weaknesses. To begin with, detente never provided the benefits—in terms of increased Soviet cooperation in curbing Third World upheavals—originally promised by its architects. Secondly, the Traders never provided an adequate explanation for the continued expansion of Soviet military power; while both camps recognized that Moscow's overall capabilities remained inferior to those of

*"Now there are signs of U.S. weakness
everywhere, and cracks are appearing in
the system. The policies set in motion
during the Vietnam war are now
threatening the way of life built since
World War II. The military retreat that
began with the defeat of the U.S. in a
place that held no natural resources or
markets now threatens to undermine the
nation's ability to protect the vital oil
supply and the energy base of the global
economy."*

—"The Decline of U.S. Power,"
Business Week, March 12, 1979.

the West, the Traders—betrayed by their own anti-
Communist outlook—declined to challenge the exaggerated
claims of the Prussians and thus accorded tacit endorsement
to their alarmist conclusions. Finally, by relying so heavily
on "surrogate gendarmes" like the Shah of Iran, the Traders
inevitably invited revolt against the very "pillars" of their
strategic design. With the fall of the Shah in January 1979,
the Trader position appeared fundamentally indefensible
and large numbers of policymakers defected to the Prussian
camp.

What ultimately destroyed the Trader position, however,
was not so much any particular crisis but rather a growing
sense among policymakers that the postwar global order
they helped create was breaking down, and that military
force alone could assure the survival of this order, and with
it, America's continued economic prosperity. This view,
widely propagated by dissident policymakers during the late
1970s (see Chapter II), became the dominant outlook in the
months succeeding the flight of the Shah. Thus, when
Business Week argued in March 1979 that America had to
adopt an assertive military policy to protect "the way of life
built since World War II," it was reflecting a consensus that
had already taken root in elite circles. This consensus was
reflected in statements by Secretary of Defense Brown and

8

Secretary of Energy Schlesinger to the effect that the United States was now prepared to consider "the use of military force" to protect Persian Gulf oil, and in a secret White House decision to alert U.S. forces for possible intervention in the Yemen border war of March 1979.[12]

The Brown-Schlesinger statements over oil, coupled with Carter's muscle-flexing over Yemen, were cited by observers both inside and outside the Administration as proof that official Washington had now recovered from the Vietnam Syndrome. "This country went through a very deep philosophical-cultural crisis as a result of the war in Vietnam," national security adviser Zbigniew Brzezinski acknowledged in April, but "it is now emerging from that crisis." The Administration's response to Yemen, he noted, "signalled to others that we will use force when necessary to protect our important interests."[13]

The events in Iran and Yemen also had a big impact in Congress. "The tide that swept back U.S. intervention in Vietnam, Cambodia, and Angola could now be turning the other way," *The Washington Post* reported in June. "Strong pressures are beginning to build up that could pave the way for a return to a more interventionist policy, based on military presence, to guarantee U.S. access to foreign energy supplies."[14] And in a comment that captured the mood of many in Congress, Senator Sam Nunn noted that "I'd rather flex our muscles a little bit on a weekly basis than have to resort to a great display of force at some very high level of danger."[15]

With official Washington now "recovered" from the Vietnam Syndrome, the Administration began the reconstitution of America's interventionary apparatus. In June 1979, Army Chief of Staff Gen. Bernard W. Rogers revealed plans for a "Unilateral Force"—later to be renamed the Rapid Deployment Force (RDF)—for use in combatting armed insurgencies abroad. At about the same time, the National Security Council (NSC) adopted a new strategic plan for the Persian Gulf calling for an expanded U.S. naval presence and the acquisition of additional basing facilities.[16] (See Chapters III and V.) Because the public still generally adhered to a non-interventionist stance, however, these plans were mostly kept secret until, several months later, the Iranian hostage crisis transformed public attitudes and thus permitted disclosure of the Administration's moves. But

9

while the hostage situation—and the public outcry it produced—was used by government officials to justify formation of the RDF and implementation of the NSC strategy, the
fact is that those moves had already been initiated *prior to the
Iranian crisis*, and in response to *elite* rather than public
pressure.

Nevertheless, the Iranian hostage crisis did produce a
major shift in public attitudes. In a characteristic expression
of the new mood, Democratic Party chairman John White
noted that "We may have reached a turning point in our
attitudes towards ourselves, and that is a feeling that we have
a right to protect legitimate interests anywhere in the
world."[17] This shift became even more pronounced several
weeks later, when powerful Soviet forces moved into Afghanistan. In the aftermath of the invasion, President Carter
publicly endorsed the Prussian position when, on January
23, 1980, he announced that the United States was now fully
prepared to use military force in defense of Persian Gulf oil
supplies, and that, to lend credibility to the Administration's
new stance, he would ask Congress to authorize registration
for the draft. "In terms of domestic politics," one White
House staffer noted at the time, "this has put an end to the
Vietnam Syndrome."[18]

The Triumph of
Interventionism—And the
Persistence of the Syndrome

Although Jimmy Carter finally embraced an interventionist
position in the closing months of his Administration, his
"conversion" came too late to satisfy his opponents—most
of whom (including many former Democrats) rallied to the
banner of Ronald Reagan. Throughout the campaign, Reagan denounced Carter's "vacillation" in the face of overseas
crises. In a major address to the Chicago Council on Foreign
Relations on March 17, he asserted that by following a policy
of "vacillation, appeasement, and aimlessness," Mr. Carter
was bringing dishonor and humiliation to the United States
"all over the world." Similarly, in his nomination speech of
July 17, Reagan charged that "the Carter Administration
gives us weakness when we need strength; vacillation when

10

"We may have reached a turning point in our attitude toward ourselves, and that is a feeling that we have a right to protect legitimate American interests anywhere in the world."
—Democratic Party Chairman John White, in *The New York Times*, December 2, 1979.

the times demand firmness." In place of such defeatism, Reagan promised to make the restoration of American power his "No. 1 priority."[19]

Upon entering the White House, Mr. Reagan moved swiftly to implement his hard-lined military program. His choices for Secretary of State and Defense, Alexander Haig and Caspar Weinberger, are both ideologically committed to an expanded military and an assertive posture abroad. With evident White House approval, Mr. Haig has initiated an intensive counterinsurgency campaign in El Salvador—the first of its type involving U.S. advisers since Vietnam—and Mr. Weinberger has introduced a new five-year military budget calling for an increase of $185 billion over Carter's proposed defense budget. Top Administration officials have also argued that we must expand our capacity to use force in the defense of U.S. interests abroad. Thus, in an address to the American Newspaper Publishers Association on May 5, 1981, Weinberger affirmed that we must be prepared to engage "in wars of any size and shape and in any region where we have vital interests."[20]

So far, the Administration has placed all its emphasis on expanding our *capability* for intervention abroad. This means, Secretary Weinberger explained on May 5, "developing urgently a better ability to respond to crises far from our shores, and to stay there as long as necessary" to protect key U.S. interests.[21] But anyone exposed to official thinking on these matters cannot help but conclude that Washington is equally concerned with demonstrating a will to *use* force. Thus, in defending his decision to establish a permanent U.S. military presence in the Middle East, President Reagan argued that American forces must be sufficiently visible so that potential adversaries will know "that if they made a reckless move, they would be risking a

11

"To an outsider, at least, the President and his men seem to have resurrected the thesis that we can and should play world policeman."
—Hodding Carter III,
The Wall Street Journal,
April 30, 1981.

confrontation with the United States."[22] And, as history has shown only all too often, this sort of preoccupation with "showing resolve" and "restoring credibility" can easily evolve into a decision to use force solely to demonstrate a *willingness* to do so.

For many observers, the Administration has already taken this step by moving into El Salvador in order to show, as Reagan put it on March 3, 1981, that we will "not just sit passively by and allow this hemisphere to be invaded by outside [*sic.*] forces."[23] But while the Administration clearly remains committed to a major counterinsurgency effort in El Salvador, it has not deployed U.S. combat forces there in any sort of strength. Such a show-of-force may yet occur in Central America, or could occur in some other Third World area—Libya, perhaps, or Angola or Yemen—where "vital" U.S. interests are supposedly threatened by hostile forces. Military intervention, should it occur, could take several forms, each discussed at length in the chapters which follow:

—An *"Energy War"* to protect Persian Gulf oil imports as dictated by the "Carter Doctrine," which has been fully endorsed by the Reagan Administration (see Chapters III and V).

—A *"Resource War"* to protect U.S. imports of critical minerals, as dictated by the "Haig Doctrine" (see Chapter IV).

—A *Counterinsurgency War* designed to crush a national liberation movement or urban uprising in some strategic Third World country (see Chapter VI).

—An *Overseas "Police Action"* designed to combat "terrorism" or other forms of "international turbulence" sponsored or facilitated by the Soviet Union (see Chapter II).

But while the Reagan Administration is clearly prepared

to adopt any of these scenarios, it is also fearful of another defeat like Vietnam ("never again," President Reagan declared on March 3, 1981, will we "send an active fighting force to a country to fight unless it is for a cause that we intend to win"[24]) and thus will have to choose carefully in selecting a site for U.S. intervention. For, as many recent events have demonstrated, today's world is a far different place than the world of the 1950s and early 1960s, when American power seemed essentially limitless and Third World conflicts were viewed as "brushfire wars" easily doused by American troops. Because many Third World armies are now equipped with modern aircraft, missiles, and tanks—acquired, in many cases, from the United States or its allies through the international arms market—and because the Soviet Union can now provide its allies and clients with considerable military backing (see Appendix), any U.S. intervention could result in conflict on a much larger scale and at a much higher *level of violence* than that experienced in Vietnam (see Chapter V). Such an encounter will be inherently dangerous—risking, as it does, confrontation with the U.S.S.R. and escalation to thermonuclear war—and thus will not be lightly countenanced by Washington no matter how eagerly U.S. officials seek a dramatic show-of-force in the Third World.

Ultimately, however, the greatest bar to U.S. adventurism abroad is not so much any of these military factors as the surprising persistence of the Vietnam Syndrome. True, the public would probably support military action to free U.S. citizens in the event of another hostage takeover, or to protect oil supplies in the case of a clear, identifiable threat. But most Americans remain opposed to the indiscriminate use of force to "show resolve," or to suppress nationalist guerrillas who pose no apparent threat to fundamental U.S. interests. Indeed, Congressional staffers reported in early 1981 that mail from constitutents was running twenty-to-one against U.S. intervention in El Salvador, and many religious organizations have adopted resolutions opposing the military aid to the Salvadorean junta. The Syndrome still persists, moreover, in some quarters of the Congress—and especially in the Democratic-controlled House. Thus, Rep. Stephen Solarz of the House Foreign Affairs Committee reported in February 1981 that while his colleagues were agreed on the need for increased economic aid to El   13

Salvador, "the consensus collapses when it comes to the question of whether we should provide military assistance, and it certainly collapses when it comes to the question of whether we should have military advisers in the country."[25]

Because many U.S. leaders, including top Administration officials, are determined to fully erase the Vietnam Syndrome from the public consciousness, we can expect renewed attacks on this stance in the months and years ahead. Such attacks will assume all of the forms already encountered—warnings of the overpowering "Soviet threat" to U.S. friends and allies, of the upsurge of "terrorism" and "turbulence" in the Third World, and of the growing threat to U.S. energy supplies and other strategic raw materials—and may assume still new forms—e.g., discovery of an *internal* threat to U.S. security posed by opponents of military preparedness (as suggested by selected witnesses in testimony to the newly-created Senate Subcommittee on Security and Terrorism). Nevertheless, the memories of U.S. paralysis and despair in Vietnam remain potent and, thanks to the efforts of many Vietnam War veterans and former antiwar activists, very much in the public eye. So long as these memories remain alive, and the public remains skeptical about official explanations for government conduct, the Vietnam Syndrome will continue to discourage indiscriminate military intervention abroad.

As we shall show in the pages which follow, any future intervention of the sort now being contemplated by U.S. strategists could easily lead to World War III or to a series of costly and debilitating repetitions of the original Vietnam conflict. Accordingly, this book reflects the belief that the Vietnam Syndrome—far from being an obstacle to U.S. security—embodies the very essence of our national self-interest. And because it precludes U.S. involvement in internal Third World conflicts, most of which arise from popular resistance to inequality and despotism, this stance is also fully consistent with our historical commitment to national self-determination. This book is designed, therefore, to underscore the beneficial—and patriotic—character of the Vietnam Syndrome, and to expose the risks and penalties of a revived interventionist posture.

II.
THE BROWN DOCTRINE: CURBING GLOBAL "TURBULENCE"

In presenting its case for an across-the-board, $185 billion boost in military spending over the next five years, the Reagan Administration has implied that the sole purpose of this massive buildup is to counter growing Soviet military power. "We are being forced," Secretary of Defense Caspar Weinberger testified on March 4, 1981, "into a continuing and apparently long-term military and political competition with the Soviets, and we are not maintaining a competitive position." To prevent Moscow from exploiting its growing strength, he avowed, we must "significantly and quickly strengthen our ability to respond to the Soviet threat at all levels of conflict and in all areas of the world vital to our national interest."[1] This rationale for the proposed military buildup has been largely accepted by Congress, which is expected to appropriate the funds requested by Weinberger. But while White House, Congress, and the press have all affirmed the urgency of confronting the "Soviet threat," a second, equally powerful motive appears to drive the current military buildup: the fear of uncontrolled "turbulence" in the Third World.

The "turbulence" theme has been growing in intensity since the Arab oil embargo of 1974, but has become especially conspicuous since the Iranian Revolution of 1978-79 and the hostage crisis which followed. These dramatic events gave visible substance to what had previously been a generalized anxiety: namely, that the present world order (which is assumed to be the most desirable order for all parties concerned) is increasingly threatened by growing instability in the Third World. This instability— 15

*"Military strength will not by itself
often be productive in dealing with the
basic causes of disorder in this tumultuous world. But ... in some circumstances, it may be our only recourse. We
seek peace, but in a world of disputes
and violence, we cannot afford to go
abroad unarmed."*

—Secretary of Defense Harold Brown,
Dept. of Defense Annual Report, Fiscal Year 1981.

evident in the wave of coups, rebellions, riots, and other
disorders which has swept through the Third World in the
past few years—is viewed as a vital threat to the West's
economic survival, which rests, to an ever-increasing degree, on access to markets and raw materials in these areas.
And because the United States, alone of the Western
powers, has the capacity to protect the world order against
the multiplicity of threats it presently faces, we must assume responsibility for preservation of global stability. As
expressed by Guy Pauker of the RAND Corporation in an
influential 1977 report, this outlook holds that "there is a
non-negligible chance that mankind. . . faces the breakdown
of the global order," and that the United States, "as a
superpower cast by history in a role of world leadership,"
must be prepared "to use its military force to prevent the
total collapse of the world order."[2]

This outlook, while widely shared by top U.S. policymakers, has generally been subordinated to the more com-
pelling issue of Soviet military power. In 1980, however,
Secretary of Defense Harold Brown elevated the turbulence
issue to near-parity with the Soviet threat. "International
economic disorder," he told Congress on January 27,
"could almost equal in severity the military threat from the
Soviet Union."[3] This statement, taken from Brown's Fiscal
Year 1981 report on U.S. military posture, was part of an
extended discussion of the threats to U.S. security arising
from what he called "International Turbulence." Besides
economic disorder, these threats included political and

16

social upheavals in the Third World, ethnic and religious conflicts, and various forms of insurgency, rebellion, and guerrilla warfare. "The number of unresolved international disputes increases," he observed, "and old ones continue to fester." Because these disputes threaten fundamental U.S. interests—especially oil supplies—and because they can erupt into something even more dangerous, America must play a more vigorous role in curbing global turbulence. "In a world of disputes and violence," he affirmed, "we cannot afford to go abroad unarmed."[4]

Coming at a time when most U.S. leaders were fully occupied with denunciations of the Soviet thrust into Afghanistan (which had occurred one month earlier), Brown's discussion of Third World turbulence was noteworthy both for its divergence from prevailing military doctrine, and also for its extreme pessimism on the world situation. Whereas other U.S. strategists were focused almost exclusively on the threat of a Soviet push into the Middle East, Brown saw upheavals emerging everywhere— and mostly from causes other than Soviet adventurism. "Political, economic and social grievances exist on a world-wide basis," he suggested, "and provide fertile soil for sabotage, subversion, terror, and civil war." These grievances largely stem from our inability "to provide for the basic needs of people and narrow the explosive disparity between wealth and hunger." This picture is further complicated, Brown noted, by Soviet attempts to exploit these divisions for its own political advantage. "But the Soviet Union is only part of the problem," he conceded; more important, by far, are "differences about the proper world distribution of income and natural resources."[5]

Brown's identification of "international turbulence" as a profound and *autonomous* threat to U.S. security, and his appreciation of the *structural* causes of such instability, constitute a radical—if not entirely unprecedented—departure in U.S. military thinking. And while the Reagan Administration has tended to emphasize the Soviet threat at the expense of all other security issues, the concern with global turbulence persists. Thus the Joint Chiefs of Staff (JCS) noted in their Fiscal 1982 "Military Posture Statement" that U.S. security is gravely threatened by "increased turbulence in areas of vital economic importance to us,"[6] and Secretary of State Alexander Haig told the editors of

"The escalating setbacks to our interests abroad, increasing lawlessness and terrorism, and the so-called wars of national liberation are putting in jeopardy our ability to influence world events. . . and to assure access to raw materials."
—Secretary of State Alexander Haig,
Time, March 16, 1981.

Time on March 16, 1981, that growing Third World "lawlessness" threatens U.S. access to critical raw materials.[7] Given the degree of concern over Third World instability, and the very real prospect of further conflicts in these areas, it is likely that the "turbulence" issue will play an ever more prominent role in U.S. military doctrine in the years ahead. Because, however, Secretary Brown was the first major figure to develop this theme in official documents, and because he developed the blueprints for a U.S. military response, it is appropriate to describe U.S. efforts to curb global unrest as the "Brown Doctrine."[8]

At the core of this doctrine is a profound appreciation of America's growing dependence on foreign markets and sources of raw materials. "The particular manner in which our economy has expanded," Brown explained in 1980, "means that we have come to depend to no small degree on imports, exports, and the earnings from overseas investments for our material well-being." Of such dependencies, none is greater than that on Middle Eastern oil supplies: "A large-scale disruption in the supply of foreign oil," he observed, "could have as damaging consequences for the United States as the loss of an important military campaign, or indeed a war."[9] (See Chapter III for a discussion of U.S. efforts to protect the oil flow from the Middle East.) Besides oil, U.S. officials—especially Secretary of State Haig—also worry about the supply of chromium, nickel, cobalt, and other critical minerals not found in abundance in the United States (see Chapter IV).

Compounding the problem of dependence is the fact that many critical materials are found in areas suffering from

18

political unrest and armed conflict. This is most apparent, of course, in the Middle East where, according to Brown, "war, terrorism, and subversion" threaten "temporary disruptions or a more permanent decline in the supply of oil."[10] Similar conditions also prevail in southern Africa, source of much of the West's chromium, manganese, cobalt, and plantimum, and in other resource-rich Third World areas. Because continued unrest in these areas could threaten U.S. access to critical materials and invite Soviet intervention, the United States must, in the view of top U.S. policymakers, use military force to protect key economic interests. "Military strength will not by itself often be productive in dealing with the basic causes of disorder in this tumultuous world," Brown affirmed, but "in some circumstances it may be our only recourse."[11]

Indisputably the earliest key figure to identify global "turbulence" as a major threat to U.S. security, Harold Brown was also the first to propose a specific remedy: the Rapid Deployment Force (RDF). Originally proposed in 1977 when U.S. strategists conceded that existing forces were inadequate to protect U.S. economic interests on a worldwide basis, the RDF has since grown into an established force with elaborate headquarters facilities and "draw down" rights over 300,000 Army, Navy, Marine, and Air Force personnel (See Chapter V). At the outbreak of future crises, these troops will be rushed overseas on jumbo transport planes and sent directly into battle with a full range of modern combat gear. Creation of the RDF, Brown declared in 1980, will enable us "to move forces of appropriate size quickly over long distances to deter or, if necessary, to defeat threats to our vital interests."[12]

Looking Back: Origins of the "Brown Doctrine"

For students of U.S. foreign policy, much of this—including the proposed solution—will appear vaguely familiar. In the late 1950s, critics of the Eisenhower Administration's "Massive Retaliation" policy argued that nuclear war did not constitute a credible deterrent to anything other than an all-out Soviet assault on the United States. In *The Uncertain Trumpet*, General Maxwell Taylor asserted that many "limited wars which have occurred since 1945—the Chinese civil war, the guerrilla warfare in Greece and Malaya, Vietnam, Taiwan, Hungary, the Middle East, Laos, to mention only a few—are clear evidence that, while our massive retaliatory strategy may have prevented the Great War—a World War III—it has not maintained the Little Peace: that is, peace from disturbances which are little only in comparison with the disaster of general war."[13] This argument was also advanced by the Senate Foreign Relations Committee in an influential 1957 study of the foreign aid program. In its final report, the Committee charged that Massive Retaliation's "exclusive focus on Soviet-initiated action ignores the real possibility that the two-thirds of the world's population outside the Iron Curtain just emerging into political and economic awareness may become an *independent source of turbulence and change*," with far-reaching consequences for U.S. security.[14] (Emphasis added.)

These concerns are very much to the fore when the Rockefeller Brothers Fund commissioned Henry Kissinger, then a professor at Harvard, to prepare a position paper on military policy in the 1960s. In his report, Kissinger argued that "even if we succeed in deterring all-out war by the threat of total annihilation," America will remain in peril because "we cannot expect to counter limited military challenges by the response appropriate to all-out surprise attack." To complement our retaliatory capabilities, therefore, "it is imperative that. . . we develop units that can intervene rapidly and that are able to make their power felt with discrimination and versatility."[15]

The concept of a rapid intervention force for use in countering Third World upheavals was adopted with considerable enthusiasm by the incoming Kennedy Administration. In protecting ourselves against the growing threat of "national liberation movements," then Secretary of Defense Robert S. McNamara explained, America has two choices: "Either we can station numbers of men and quantities of equipment and supplies overseas near all potential trouble spots, or we can maintain a much smaller force in a central reserve in the United States and deploy it rapidly where needed." Given the enormous costs of the former approach, establishment of "a mobile 'fire brigade' reserve, centrally located. . . and ready for quick deployment to any threatened area in the world is, basically, a more economical and flexible use of our military forces."[16]

To provide this "fire brigade" with the necessary global mobility, McNamara and Taylor (then Chairman of the Joint Chiefs of Staff) proposed the acquisition of two new vehicles: the giant C-5A transport plane, and the Fast Deployment Logistics (FDL) ship. In its initial enthusiasm for the quick-strike policy, Congress voted $3 billion for the C-5A (later raised to $6 billion to overcome persistent "cost overruns" encountered by the builder, Lockheed Aircraft).[17] By the time the FDL proposal came up for a vote, however, America was deeply embroiled in Vietnam and many lawmakers had begaun to repudiate the policies that had led to our involvement in that conflict. "Beyond the cost," the Senate Armed Services Committee affirmed in a report criticizing the FDL, "the Committee is concerned about the possible creation of an impression that the United States has assumed the function of policing the world." Senator Richard B. Russell, then chairman of the Committee and normally a reliable supporter of military programs, further charged that by facilitating Pentagon planning for future interventions, the FDL would make such adventures all the more likely. "If it is easy for us to go anywhere and do anything," he told his colleagues in the Senate, "then we will always be going somewhere and doing something."[18]

As America disengaged from Vietnam, opposition to a "go anywhere, do anything" stance was institutionalized in the War Powers Act and other legislative constraints on presidential war-making abroad. The prevailing mood of non-interventionism, widely characterized as the "Vietnam Syndrome," forced Washington to seek alternative mechanisms for protecting critical interests abroad. Under the Nixon Doctrine, favored U.S. allies such as Iran were converted into "surrogate gendarmes" and charged with the responsibility of "maintaining order" in critical Third World areas. And, as the local "peacekeeping" function was shifted to other powers, U.S. military leaders resurrected their original Cold War mission—defense of Western Europe against Soviet attack—as the principal rationale for higher military spending.

For most of the 1970s, U.S. war planning concentrated

"As the leading affluent 'have' power, we may expect to have to fight for our national valuables against envious 'have-nots."
—Gen. Maxwell D. Taylor,
Foreign Affairs, April, 1974.

on hypothetical East-West conflicts in Europe, while Third World contingencies were accorded relatively little attention. The new NATO emphasis was widely endorsed in Washington, both because it avoided any hint of interventionism, and because it assured bipartisan support for sustained military spending. But, just as dissident strategists had questioned the exclusive anti-Soviet orientation of Massive Retaliation in the 1950s, some U.S. leaders began to question the similar focus of U.S. war planning in the 1970s. Arguing that U.S. economic survival was more than ever dependent on access to overseas markets and raw materials, these strategists campaigned to reverse the "Vietnam Syndrome" and to rehabilitate intervention as a legitimate means for coping with renewed "turbulence" in the Third World.

Ironically, one of the first military figures to challenge the new orthodoxy was Maxwell Taylor, the leader of the original revolt against Massive Retaliation. In a prophetic 1974 article in *Foreign Affairs*, Taylor suggested that while an East-West war in Europe has a "low probability rating" (because both sides share such an overwhelming interest in preservation of the status quo), America will increasingly be threatened by "turbulent and disorderly" conditions in the Third World. "As the leading affluent 'have' power," he affirmed, *"we may expect to have to fight for our national valuables against envious 'have-nots.'"* (Emphasis added.) To prepare for such contingencies, Taylor advanced the same posture as he had pioneered in the 1950s: "In the troubled world which I have postulated . . . , we shall need mobile, ready forces to deter or, in some cases, suppress such conflicts before they expand into something greater."[19]

Although anathema to many policymakers in the immediate post-Vietnam era, such thinking gained considerable favor among those strategists who viewed the "North-

22

> *"There is a non-negligible chance that mankind is entering a period of increased social instability and faces the possibility of a breakdown of global order as a result of a sharpening confrontation between the Third World and the industrial democracies."*
>
> —Guy Pauker, *Military Implications of a Possible World Order Crisis in the 1980s.*

South" conflict—i.e., the struggle for control of the world's resources between the advanced industrial powers (the "North") and the underdeveloped countries of the Third World (the "South")—as the most explosive threat to long-term U.S. security. This outlook was given further articulation in a widely-discussed 1977 RAND Corporation report by counterinsurgency expert Guy Pauker on "Military Implications of a Possible World Order Crisis in the 1980s." There is a growing likelihood, Pauker warned, "that mankind is entering a period of increased social instability and faces the possibility of a breakdown of global order as a result of sharpening confrontation between the Third World and the industrial democracies." This confrontation, he explained, is principally due to the inescapable fact that "the gap between rich and poor countries is so wide that no solution satisfactory to both sides is likely to emerge" at any foreseeable point. As domestic pressures mount in the poor countries for immediate and radical solutions, "the North-South conflict . . . could get out of hand in ways comparable to the peasant rebellions that in past centuries engulfed large parts of Europe or Asia, spreading like uncontrolled prairie fires." And because only the United States has the military capacity to contain and control these conflagrations, it will "be expected to use its military force to prevent the total collapse of the world order or, at least, to protect specific interests of American citizens."[20]

While many U.S. leaders eventually came to share this outlook, support for NATO remained the dominant theme

23

during most of the Carter period. In the late 1970s, however, several events occurred which irrevocably altered Washington's stance on the use of military power abroad. The first was the Iranian Revolution of 1978-79, which toppled the Shah and thus shattered the Nixon Doctrine approach of relying on surrogate gendarmes to police the Third World. At the same time, disruptions in the supply of Iranian oil helped create a severe "energy crisis" in the United States, and thus demonstrated once again how dependent we had become on imported petroleum. As a result of these two developments, the Administration officially disavowed the "Vietnam Syndrome" and affirmed that America was now prepared to employ its own forces in defense of Mideast oil supplies. "The United States has vital interests in the Persian Gulf," Energy Secretary James Schlesinger declared in February 1979, and it "must move in such a way that it protects those interests, even if that involves the use of military strength or of military presence."[21]

At first, Administration leaders sought to restrict the application of this principle to specific threats against U.S. oil supplies. But continuing unrest in the Middle East and Africa, coupled with increasingly conspicuous Soviet involvement in Ethiopia and Afghanistan, led to growing pressure for a more activist U.S. military posture. In March 1979, *Business Week* published its special issue on "The Decline of American Power," which summarized the revanchest outlook shared by many business and political leaders. While citing the growth of Soviet military power as a serious threat, the issue concentrated on the economic perils of continued U.S. reluctance to serve as the world's policeman. "The military retreat that began with the U.S. defeat in a place [Vietnam] that held no natural resources of markets now threatens to undermine the nation's ability to protect the vital oil supply and the energy base of the global economy." Echoing Taylor's "haves vs. have-nots" doctrine, the magazine suggested that we must undertake a "reassertion of U.S. influence around the world" in order to preserve "the way of life built since World War II."[22]

These views were already widely held in Congress and the media when militant Iranian students seized the U.S. embassy in Teheran. With that action, and subsequent scares of a new oil crunch, the strategic pendulum shifted away

"The American people, I think, are convinced now that U.S. military capability is not the principal source of unhappiness in the world or instability in the world and that we need to be militarily strong."

—Secretary of Defense Harold Brown,
The Pentagon, December 14, 1979.

from NATO and towards a renewed commitment to curbing "turbulence" in the Third World. Among the many U.S. lawmakers who embraced this new stance was Senator Frank Church, then chairman of the Foreign Relations Committee, who told *The New York Times*: "The highly volatile and predictable politics of the Middle East, the wave of hysteria in the Islamic world, [and] the explosive possibilities of countries like Saudi Arabia and Iraq," have all produced a belief that "we must be prepared to take action to protect vital interests."[23]

Two months later, Defense Secretary Brown issued his Fiscal 1981 annual report which formally identified "international turbulence" as a major threat to U.S. security. For the past three years, he told reporters at a press conference devoted to the report, we have concentrated on programs designed to enhance U.S. capabilities "to fight a war in Europe," while "this year we have concentrated special attention and resources on the improvement of capabilities to get personnel and equipment quickly to potential trouble areas like the Middle East, Persian Gulf, and Arabian Sea areas."[24] Reading through the report, one is continually struck by similarities to the earlier pronouncements of Maxwell Taylor, Robert McNamara, Guy Pauker, and other strategists of the Kennedy era. Thus, in a passage reminiscent of the Pauker report, Brown spoke of the many "troubles lying around like dry timber," and lamented that "despite our needs and preferences, we cannot now count on world stability."[25]

Brown's proposed responses to these threats are also reminiscent of the Kennedy era. The Rapid Deployment Force is nothing but a modern incarnation of McNamara's

25

"In the troubled world which I have postulated, minor wars are very probable, although unpredictable as to specifics. We shall need mobile, ready forces to deter or, in some cases, suppress such conflicts before they expand into something greater. This task is the primary justification for an uncommitted central reserve in the United States ready for presidential use as an instrument of national policy."

—Gen. Maxwell D. Taylor,
Foreign Affairs, April, 1974.

"fire brigade," and like the Special Forces before it, will serve as a general-purpose strike force for suppressing unforeseen disturbances abroad. To whisk these forces overseas and to supply them with all necessary combat gear, Brown proposed two initiatives in the Fiscal 1981 budget: a new intercontinental transport plane dubbed the C-X, and a fleet of arms-laden cargo vessels known as "maritime pre-positioning ships" (MPS) which will be stationed near potential troublespots in the Indian Ocean, the Mediterranean, and the Arabian Sea. The C-X is, of course, nothing but an updated version of the C-5A, while the MPS is for all intents and purposes a facsimile of McNamara's FDL vessels.

Even the deployment strategy remains the same: at the onset of a crisis, the "fire brigade" (now the RDF) will be flown on C-5As (and eventually on the C-X) to friendly airports near the combat zone, where they will pick up their heavy equipment from the FDL (MPS) and then move off to the battlefield. (See Chapter V). And, as in McNamara's time, getting to the battlefield *quickly* is very important: "Our needs in responding to non-NATO crises," Brown told reporters in 1979, "center on our ability to move available forces over vast distances quickly enough, either to deter conflict or, if that's not successful, to prevail in conflict."[26]

This emphasis on *getting there quickly* is one of the most ominous features of the RDF concept. It derives, of course, from the Vietnam experience: the Pentagon is naturally terrified of a protracted conflict in the Third World that would provoke widespread opposition at home, and thus in future crises U.S. forces will be rushed overseas in order to dominate the battlefield quickly so as (in Maxwell Taylor's words) "to suppress such conflicts before they expand into something greater." But whatever the impetus for this policy, it obviously suggests a "hair-trigger" stance in which American forces would be sent overseas at the first sign of a crisis. Such a stance would, moreover, be consistent with the Pentagon's view that the RDF may be used to "deter" conflict—by physically occupying the battlefield before the battle gets fully underway—as well as to counter aggression by others. As explained by RDF Commander Gen. P.X. Kelley in 1980, this "pre-emptive strategy" holds that "once you get a force into an area that is not occupied by the other guy, then you have changed the whole calculus of the crisis, and he must react to you, and you not to him."[27]

It doesn't take much imagination to recognize that such a "first strike" posture could prove a shortcut to catastrophe. It might, in some cases, force the "other guy" to back down—but it might just as easily result in a major conflagration that could otherwise have been prevented. And because such a conflagration could involve direct conflict with Soviet or Soviet-backed forces, it is painfully obvious that we could find ourselves in the opening engagements of World War III. (See Chapter V for further discussion of Kelley's "pre-emptive strategy"—and its risks.)

Even if they don't lead to World War III, however, U.S. efforts to curb global "turbulence" could prove disastrous to the United States. To begin with, such efforts will be very, very expensive: start-up costs of the Rapid Deployment Force, for instance, are estimated at $20-$25 billion, and acquisition of all the added ships and aircraft needed to support the RDF overseas could cost another $50-$100 billion (includes the cost of a new "Fifth Fleet" for permanent deployment in the Indian Ocean area). And because the present, all-volunteer military system is not producing sufficient "bodies" for the expanded police force envisioned by the Brown Doctrine, it is highly likely that the Reagan

> *"The use of military force is not, and should not be, a desirable American policy response to the internal politics of other nations. We believe we have the right to shape our future; we must respect that right in others."*
> —Cyrus Vance, Commencement Address, Harvard University, June 5, 1980.

Administration will move eventually towards reinstatement of the draft.[28]

All of this will require major "sacrifices" (as Reagan would have it) by the American public: cutbacks in social spending, increased inflation, declining living standards, and possible exposure to conscription. And because a more assertive military posture abroad is likely to provoke considerable dissent at home—as demonstrated by the outcry over U.S. involvement in El Salvador—we can also expect some increase in political repression. There is also an immeasurable but not negligible *moral* cost: by becoming policeman to the world, we automatically surrender our claim to be defenders of national self-determination and other libertarian principles. "We believe we have the right to shape our future," former Secretary of State Cyrus Vance told graduating students at Harvard University in June, 1980, and thus "we must respect that right in others."[29]

We would also pay a price in our international relations. While some petty dictators would undoubtedly applaud U.S. efforts to preserve the *status quo*, most Third World governments would be forced to condemn U.S. "police" actions abroad. The experience of colonialism is too recent, and the commitment to national sovereignty too great, to permit any truly independent government to endorse U.S. military intervention—any more than such governments could endorse the Soviet invasion of Afghanistan. Indeed, it is likely that the principal beneficiary of such action would be the U.S.S.R., which could thereby hope to repair the damage caused by Afghanistan and pose again as the principal defender of the Third World in its resistance to imperialism. In the Middle East, for instance, a U.S. invasion to

28

"seize Arab oil" would, in the words of former Deputy Assistant Secretary of State James Noyes, "herald the beginning of a golden Middle East era for the Soviet Union."[30]

Finally, there is not a shred of hope that U.S. efforts to curb global turbulence through military action will result in any permanent decline in Third World violence. Because, as Secretary Brown himself admitted, the principal cause of such turbulence is our failure "to provide for the basic needs of people," and military action simply cannot "be productive in dealing with the basic causes of disorder in this tumultuous world." In fact, it is only all too likely that U.S. intervention will produce wounds and resentments that will actually *increase* the threat to global security. "We must ultimately recognize," Secretary Vance declared at Harvard, "that the demand for individual freedom cannot be long repressed without sowing the seeds of violent convulsion."[31] Perhaps the RDF could succeed in containing a conflict here or (temporarily) suppressing a rebellion there—but it will never address the fundamental causes of instability, and thus we will find ourselves in a succession of costly and debilitating interventions that will surely end in the financial and moral bankruptcy of our nation.

III.
THE CARTER DOCTRINE:
"ENERGY WARS"
IN THE MIDDLE EAST

For years, U.S. military planning concentrated on the two perceived nodes of East-West conflict: Europe and the Far East. Now, as a result of the energy crisis and growing superpower encroachments, a third area has come to monopolize the attention of U.S. strategists: the oil-rich Persian Gulf region. On January 23, 1980, following a series of upheavals in the region, President Carter formally defined the Gulf as an area of major military importance to the United States. "Let our position be absolutely clear," he told a joint session of Congress: "An attempt by any outside force to gain control of the Persian Gulf region will be regarded as an assault on the vital interests of the United States," and will thus "be repelled with any means necessary, including military force."[1] This declaration, immediately dubbed the "Carter Doctrine," has since been reaffirmed by the Reagan Administration and now figures as the principal rationale for expansion of the U.S. war machine. And while other crises may periodically deflect Washington's attention, it is apparent that planning for conflicts over Mideast oil supplies—or for what might best be called "energy wars"—will remain the consuming Pentagon concern.

Energy wars are not, of course, an entirely new phenomenon. In the 19th and early twentieth centuries, the European powers contended with one another for control of African and Asian lands believed to contain deposits of coal, petroleum, and other strategic raw materials. Such skirmishing was particularly prevalent in the Persian Gulf area following the discovery of oil in 1908, and many historians believe that the outcome of the first two World Wars was significantly

Area of U.S. Concern in the Middle East and Western Asia

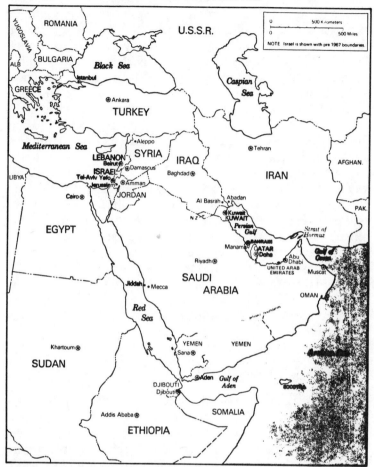

Source: Congressional Budget Office.

affected by the struggle over Middle Eastern oil supplies. But the situation we face today is, in the view of most analysts, qualitatively different. Because *so much* of the world's available energy supplies is concentrated in Mideast oilfields—an estimated two-thirds of free world petroleum reserves—modern industrial civilization as we know it could collapse if all these supplies were obstructed or destroyed. Given these stakes, it is unlikely that any future "energy wars" in the Middle East will resemble the sideshows of the past years. "If there is another world war," OPEC President Mana Saeed Al-Otaiba said recently, "it will be over petroleum."[2]

If talk of a world war over oil appears excessively alarmist to some, it does not to those responsible for planning America's future military posture. "Protection of the oil flow from the Middle East is clearly part of our vital interest," former Defense Secretary Harold Brown declared in 1979, and "in protection of those vital interests we'll take any action that's appropriate, including the use of military force."[3] To provide Washington with the capacity to overcome any threat to Mideast oil, Brown established the 200,000-man Rapid Deployment Force (RDF) and initiated negotiations for the establishment of RDF bases in the Middle East. This force would rely initially on conventional weapons, but Pentagon officials acknowledge that "we are thinking of theater nuclear options" should non-nuclear measures prove inadequate.[4] U.S. war planners also talk—albeit not quite so openly—of "seizing Arab oil" in the event of another embargo or unacceptable price increases. Because any of these measures could trigger a global conflagration, it is essential that we look closely at the justifications for going to war over oil, and to ask whether, indeed, there are other ways to assure our continued access to adequate energy supplies.

The Oil "Jugular"

To a large degree, the risk of energy wars in the Middle East is the result of what has been called an "accident of geography:" instead of being scattered randomly across the globe, the world's largest deposits of recoverable petroleum are located in a handful of desert tracts surrounding the 600-mile long Persian Gulf.* On a normal day, these fields produce some 22 million barrels of crude oil, or about one-third of total Free World consumption. Most of this petroleum is carried by tanker across the Gulf and through the Strait of Hormuz into the Indian Ocean, and thence to refineries in Europe, Japan, North America, and other oil-consuming areas. Because so much of our industry runs on

---

*It has long been common in Western circles to call this body of water the "Persian Gulf." However, it is also called the "Arabian Gulf" by nations occupying its western and southern shores. Wherever possible, we will simply call it "the Gulf," but to avoid confusion, we will use the common Western name when a choice is necessary.

oil, and because so much of it comes from this one remote locale, the Strait of Hormuz has been called the free world's "jugular" and its protection considered a matter of economic life and death. "The umbilical cord of the Western World," Defense Secretary Caspar Weinberger avowed on March 4, 1981, "runs through the Strait of Hormuz into the Arabian Gulf and the nations which surround it."[5]

And the oil jugular is vulnerable. Not only are Russian troops poised several hundred miles away in Afghanistan and Central Asia, but the Gulf area itself is torn by long-standing political, religious, and economic conflicts. Border disputes and other interstate rivalries are legion: Iran vs. Iraq, Iraq vs. Kuwait, North Yemen vs. South Yemen, South Yemen vs. Oman, and the Arab world as a whole vs. Israel. "As if this were not enough," Secretary Brown wrote in 1980, "the region is shaken by ethnic, religious, and internal political divisions."[6] Iran remains in a state of "revolutionary chaos," and Saudi Arabia was shaken to its Muslim foundations by the 1979 rebel attack on Mecca. Furthermore, the employment of large numbers of foreign workers—many of them Palestinians—has introduced still other disputes to the Gulf area. As demonstrated by the Iran-Iraq war of 1980-81, any of these local conflicts or rivalries can erupt in armed conflict, thereby threatening the oil production and inviting superpower involvement. Once hostilities commenced, moreover, it would be extremely difficult to contain the fighting and to assure the continued flow of oil.

Given the high stakes involved and the potential for catastrophe, protection of Mideast oil supplies has long been a major concern of U.S. military planners. Until last year, however, the close-up defense role had been relegated to Iran, which, under leadership of the Shah, had agreed to serve as the "guardian and protector" of the Gulf once British forces departed in 1971. In return for serving as America's watchdog, Tehran was invited to purchase America's most advanced and versatile weapons, and was showered with praise from the White House.[7] It is hardly surprising, therefore, that the dissidents who toppled the Pahlavi Dynasty in 1979 vowed that Iran would never again serve as surrogate "gendarmes" in the Persian Gulf.

The departure of the Shah forced Washington to conduct its first major review of Gulf area policy since then Prime

Minister Harold Wilson announced in late 1968 that Great Britain would no longer serve as regional policeman. But while that earlier review, undertaken by Henry Kissinger, resulted in a decision to rely on local forces for regional security, the Carter Administration study, directed by Zbigniew Brzezinski, concluded that the United States must be prepared to perform a direct military role in the Gulf. In June 1979, the White House announced that Administration leaders had reached consensus on the need for a beefed-up U.S. military presence, including a major expansion of U.S. naval forces in the region. Animating this effort was the belief, summarized by Mr. Brzezinski in an address to the Economic Club of Chicago, that the Middle East has become of equal strategic importance to the United States as Western Europe and the Far East, and that "a threat to the security of any one is an automatic threat to the security of the other two."[8]

Planning for a stepped-up U.S. military presence in the Gulf was already well underway in November, when militant Iranian students seized the American embassy in Teheran and touched off a new Mideast crisis. Although not directly a threat to U.S. energy supplies, the embassy takeover intensified the instability of the Gulf region and highlighted the difficulties America faces in protecting the oil flow. Thus, while Carter relied on diplomatic and economic pressures to resolve the hostage crisis itself, he also ordered a massive expansion of U.S. air and naval forces in the region and ordered the pentagon to speed up development of the Rapid Deployment Force.

More important than any of these crisis-oriented measures, however, was the shift of public attitudes toward the use of military force itself. Leaders of both major parties affirmed that the hostage crisis spelled the end of the Vietnam Syndrome, and that Washington could thenceforth expect widespread public support for a more assertive military posture abroad. As noted by John White, National Chairman of the Democratic Party, most U.S. leaders concluded that "we have a right to protect legitimate American interests anywhere in the world."[9]

With this sort of mandate, Pentagon strategists accelerated planning for an expanded U.S. military presence in the Gulf area. On December 27, 1979, Secretary Brown formally activated the RDF headquarters at MacDill Air Force

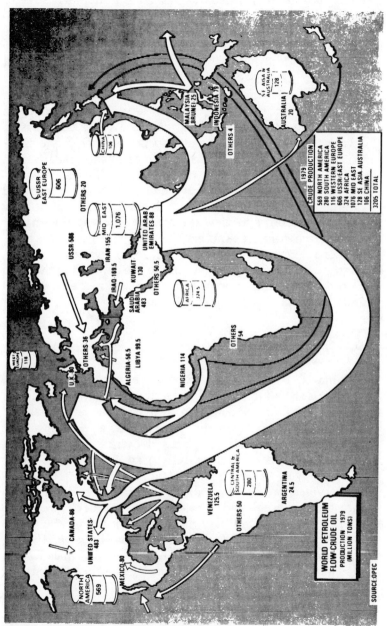

Joint Chiefs of Staff *Military Posture for* FY 1982.

Base, Fla., and reaffirmed the U.S. commitment to use force in the defense of critical overseas interests. "The Iranian situation is one of a number of events that remind us," he told reporters at MacDill, "that we have to be able to move forces quickly," either "to deter conflict, or if that's not successful, to prevail in conflict."[10]

A few hours after Brown uttered these words, Russian troops poured into Afghanistan and Southwest Asia again became the focus of world attention. While the Russian invasion naturally affected all aspects of U.S.-Soviet relations, its most immediate consequence was the redefinition of U.S. strategic policy in the Persian Gulf area. Whereas earlier planning for energy wars in the Gulf had concentrated on the threat of insurgency and border conflict, it now became necessary to view the area as a potential arena for superpower conflict. And because U.S. interests in the area are considered so critical, the Gulf region was elevated—in strategic terms—to a major defense area requiring the kind of military commitment we had already made to NATO and the countries of Northeast Asia.

The "Carter Doctrine" Controversy

The new U.S. posture was formally enunciated in Carter's January 23rd address, which described Persian Gulf oil as a "vital interest" to be defended with "any means necessary." But while this statement established a new strategic principle—the so-called "Carter Doctrine"—it raised as many questions as it appeared to answer: at what point would Soviet or other enemy action precipitate a U.S. military response? What about the (far more immediate) threat of internal and intra-regional conflict? Are there alternatives to a military-oriented posture in the Gulf? Despite the gravity of these questions, however, public attention has focused on the more narrow question of *capability*: does the United States have the capacity to defend Gulf oil supplies in response to a concerted Soviet drive to dominate the area?

Characteristic of this narrower debate were statements by some U.S. lawmakers questioning America's ability to move large U.S. forces to the Gulf quickly enough to counter a Soviet invasion. One of the Administration's

36

"Let our position be absolutely clear: An attempt by any outside force to gain control of the Persian Gulf region will be regarded as an assault on the vital interests of the United States of America, and such an assault will be repelled by any means necessary, including military force."

—President Jimmy Carter,
State of the Union address, January 23, 1980.

most persistent critics, Sen. Henry Jackson of Washington, asked Defense Secretary Brown on January 31, "whether it's wise to lay down a doctrine when there is serious doubt whether it can be upheld."[11]

In response, top Pentagon officials made numerous trips to Capitol Hill to assure Congressional leaders that the United States can in fact project substantial military power in the Gulf in enough time to make a difference. "The first aircraft could reach the region in hours," Deputy Secretary of Defense Robert Komer testified on February 21, 1980, "and the first [tactical air] wing could be operational in a matter of days." Furthermore, we have "Army units in a high degree of readiness which can, with their equipment, be lifted by air in a short time—about a week for a light brigade, about two weeks for a light division. And Marine amphibious units from outside the region could move into the region in two weeks or less." Komer conceded that Washington would have difficulty in moving heavy, tank-equipped forces into the area quickly, but insisted that the Russians would also encounter difficulties in moving heavy equipment over the mountain roads leading to the Gulf—roads which could be bombed by U.S. aircraft operating from carriers in the Arabian Sea. No one can "prejudge the outcome of such a situation," Komer told the Senate Armed Services Committee, but he affirmed that "the United States has forces that can be moved into that area quickly," and urged that "no one underestimate our capabilities to do so."[12]

U.S. officials have warned, moreover, that there is "no

37

upper limit" on the forces Washington would commit to a Persian Gulf conflict. Any threatening Soviet moves would first be met with conventional forces, reporters were told at a 1980 Pentagon press briefing, but if that proves ineffective there are "theater nuclear options" available to U.S. authorities.[13] "Any direct conflict between American and Soviet forces," Secretary Brown suggested on March 6, 1980, "carries the risk of intensification and geographical spread of the conflict. We cannot concede to the Soviets' full choice of the arena or the actions."[14]

Even these apocalyptical statements have not satisfied some policymakers, who have called for a massive expansion of U.S. forces in the area. President Reagan, who repeatedly criticized Carter's defense policies during the 1980 campaign, has pledged to give more substance to the "Carter Doctrine" by inserting a permanent military "presence" in the Gulf area. "By a presence," he told reporters on February 3, 1981, I mean that "we're there enough... for the Soviets to know that if they made a reckless move, they would be risking a confrontation with the United States." This proposal has been further developed by Defense Secretary Caspar Weinberger, who in May announced plans to convert the Rapid Deployment Force into a full-scale regional command (like the European and Pacific Commands) with responsibility for the Persian Gulf area (see Chapter V). He also announced a multi-billion dollar effort to expand U.S. "basing facilities" in the region.*

But while public debate has continued to focus on the issue of America's *capacity* to halt a hypothetical Soviet invasion, some experts have begun to question whether there is any likelihood of such a move at all. Such an "extravagant view of Soviet motivations" former Ambassador George Kennan observed in 1980, rests "exclusively on our own assumptions," for which "I am not aware of any substantiation." The Soviet invasion of Afghanistan, he

---

*As now conceived, the Pentagon plan calls for the improvement of port and airbase facilities in Oman, Egypt, Kenya and Somalia. In Oman, the U.S. will improve airbase facilities at Muscat and the Arabian Sea island of Masirah; in Egypt, the U.S. will construct new air and port facilities at Ras Banas on the Red Sea, and build "austere" barracks for any RDF forces that may be sent to the region; in Kenya, the U.S. will improve port and airport facilities at Mombasa; and in Somalia, the U.S. will upgrade the former Soviet base at Berbera.[15]

> "The umbilical cord of the industrialized free world runs through the Strait of Hormuz into the Arabian Gulf and the nations which surround it. That area, Southwest Asia and the Gulf, is and will be the fulcrum of contention for the foreseeable future."
>
> —Secretary of Defense Caspar Weinberger, Washington, March 4, 1981.

suggested, can best be explained by purely parochial concerns—e.g., "political instability in what is, after all, a border country of the Soviet Union"—rather than on some grand design for control of the Gulf.[16] This view was seconded by Keith Dunn of the Army War College, who suggested that a Soviet invasion would be "a very risky policy option and one that would seem to run counter to Moscow's historical inhibitions to take actions that might cause a direct confrontation with the United States." Any presumption of a Soviet "blueprint" for control of Mideast oilfields, moreover, is flatly contradicted by Moscow's alliance with Ethiopia—which provoked a split with Somalia and thus, according to Dunn, "damaged its geopolitical situation in the Horn of Africa and caused it to lose access to the best port facilities in the area," the deep-water port at Berbera.*[17]

Most Pentagon officials concede that there is a very low probability of a Soviet drive on the Persian Gulf. What worries them much more, in fact, is an *internal* conflict or regional dispute that jeopardizes the flow of oil. "Potential points of conflict," the Joint Chiefs of Staff warned in 1981, "abound in the region," thus raising fears of future local conflicts like the Iraq-Iran war of 1980-81. Furthermore, "frustrated expectations among the masses and emerging new elites also serve to stimulate unrest," and "the forces of Islamic resurgence and radical nationalism" can, in some

*The case for a Soviet "blueprint" for domination of Mideast oilfields was further discredited in May 1981, when the CIA discarded earlier estimates of a Soviet oil shortfall in the 1980's—which many analysts suggested might lead to Russian intervention—and concluded instead that Moscow will be able to meet its energy needs from domestic production. (*The New York Times*, May 19, 1981.)

cases, threaten Western oil supplies.[18] And while possible U.S. responses to a hypothetical Soviet attack have been widely explored, there is much more uncertainty over what steps Washington could or would take in the event of a localized conflict.

In a clearcut case of aggression by Soviet-backed forces against a U.S. ally (say South Yemen vs. Oman, or Iraq vs. Saudi Arabia), a U.S. military response would be, at this point, almost automatic. As Secretary Brown affirmed in 1980, "We need to be able to come quickly and with decisive force to the aid of allies and friends in the area. . . so as to deter, and if necesssary, defeat military incursions from outside."[19] Indeed, an examination of recent U.S. military exercises—particularly those involving forces committed to the RDF—suggest that this sort of scenario is precisely the kind of conflict Pentagon strategists are best equipped to plan for.*

What if, however, the threat were *internal?* Here U.S. policy is far more ambiguous. Presumably, Washington would come to the aid of the Saudi ruling family if it were menaced by an isolated insurgent force. But what if—as could easily happen—the Saudi family itself split up into rival groupings? In such a case, U.S. leaders would be faced with the painful choice of remaining disengaged while Saudi Arabia is torn apart, or of choosing between rival forces and thus risk being drawn into a bitter civil war. Nor is this the only upheaval with which U.S. planners must contend: a strike by foreign laborers in Kuwait or Saudi Arabia could trigger a generalized insurrection, or renewed religious strife—such as that experienced recently in Iran—could spread to other countries in the Gulf. Any of these upheavals could threaten Mideast production, and thus prompt Washington to consider military action to protect the oil flow. And depending on the circumstances, such action could involve a minor "peacekeeping" operation (say to prevent a radical takeover in one of the smaller sheikhdoms), or a

---

*During Operation "MABEX-81," for instance, U.S. forces were theoretically sent to the Persian Gulf area to help defend a pro-U.S. country, "Kinorb," against the Moscow-backed "Peoples' Republic of Elon." Observers at the exercise, held in January 1981 at Twenty-Nine Palms Marine Corps Base in southeastern California, instinctively characterized "Elon" and "Kinorb" as surrogates for South Yemen and Oman or North Yemen.[20]

prolonged counterguerrilla war (against, for instance, radical separatists in Dhofar province of Oman).

In all of the official scenarious, it is assumed that a friendly government comes under attack by hostile forces and requests American assistance. But U.S. strategists have always considered (albeit discreetly) what might happen if the Saudis *themselves* threatened U.S. interests—by ordering a new oil embargo, by posting unacceptable price increases or by aligning with radical Arab forces in an attack on Israel—and the United States moved to *seize Arab oil fields* in the face of local opposition. Such contingencies do not, of course, figure in official Pentagon statements and documents. But the concept of "seizing Arab oil" has always been present, and has risen to the surface each time the Saudis have raised oil prices or threatened collective action against Israel. And while such moves are not, at the moment, especially likely, it is obvious that consideration of an oil intervention is not about to be abandoned and is, in fact, likely to loom larger as U.S. dependence on Mideast oil increases.

"Seizing Arab Oil"

"Why don't we just send in the Marines and solve the energy crisis permanently?" Such thoughts were expressed at many a cocktail party following the fourfold OPEC price increase of 1974. It was Henry Kissinger, however, who first gave official sanction to such speculation. Asked by *Business Week* on January 1, 1975, if Washington would consider military action in response to another round of price increases, Secretary Kissinger replied that "it is one thing to use it in the case of a dispute over price"—a dispute which could be settled through negotiation—but "it's another where there is *some actual strangulation of the industrialized world.*"[21] (Emphasis added.)

Kissinger's remarks provoked an immediate storm of controversy in the Middle East. (President Anwar el-Sadat of Egypt, for instance, warned that Arab producers "would blow up oil wells" in response to such a move.) In the successive weeks, Kissinger sought to soften criticism by insisting he had no specific contingencies in mind. "The sentence that has attracted so much attention," he told Bill Moyers on January 15, "is too frequently taken totally out of   41 context." But however qualified, Kissinger's statement established a rationale for military action against the Arab oil producers. In succeeding weeks, this position was given further emphasis in statements by President Ford and Secretary of Defense James R. Schlesinger. Referring to an earlier endorsement of Kissinger's remarks, Ford told reporters on January 23, 1975, that "I wanted it made as clear as I possibly could that this country in case of economic strangulation—and the key word is 'strangulation'—we had to be prepared, without specifying what we might do, to take the necessary action for our self-preservaton."[22] Schlesinger was even more emphatic: he told *U.S. News & World Report* in May 1975 that "we might not remain entirely passive to the imposition of [another oil] embargo. I'm not going to indicate any prospective reaction other than to point out that there are economic, political, and conceivably military measures in response."[23]

If Ford and Schlesinger were hesitant to spell out what such measures were likely to entail, other analysts were not so inhibited. In a much-quoted article in the January 1975 issue of *Commentary*, Prof. Robert W. Tucker of Johns Hopkins University argued that military action might be necessary to prevent America from "bleeding to death" through "the vast financial drain resulting from present oil prices." To prevent any further "hemorrhaging," Tucker proposed that the United States occupy the area extending "from Kuwait down along the coastal region of Saudi Arabia to Qatar." This coastal strip, he continued, "has no substantial centers of population and is without trees," thus its occupation by U.S. forces would present none of the impediments found in Vietnam. And because this area harbors some 50 percent of total OPEC reserves, its control by the United States would "break the present price structure by breaking the core of the cartel politically and economically."[24]

By bringing such proposals out into the open, Tucker, who had previously opposed expanding U.S. military commitments abroad, legitimated a much wider discussion of such scenarios. Within weeks, the American press was full of articles on the feasibility of oil interventions. In the March 1975 issue of *Harper's*, "Miles Ignotus" (the pseudonym of a Washington-based defense analyst) expanded Tucker's thesis by calling outright for a U.S. action to seize Arab oil

42

fields. "The only feasible countervailing power to OPEC's control of oil is power itself—military power." Should the Arabs declare a new embargo or otherwise threaten the economic survival of the West, "force must be used selectively to occupy large and concentrated oil reserves, which can be produced rapidly in order to end the artificial scarcity of oil and thus cut the price."[25]

Like Tucker, Ignotus suggested that the best locale for such action would be Saudi Arabia, with proven reserves of 200 billion barrels. "If Vietnam was full of trees and brave men, and the national interest was almost invisible, here there are no trees, very few men, and a clear objective." While this argument has led most amateur strategists to choose Saudi Arabia as the site of such action, other possible sites have also been suggested. Some thinkers have pointed to Libya (proven reserves: 25 billion barrels) as a potential takeover target, or Kuwait, Qatar and the United Arab Emirates (total reserves: 120 billion barrels). But whichever site is chosen, the logic remains the same: "When the very existence of an international economic system is put in jeopardy by the [economic] aggression of Arab oil states," Col. Robert D. Heinl Jr. wrote in *Human Events*, "we are morally as much at war as after Pearl Harbor," and thus a fully "warlike" response is justified.[26]

In responding to such proposals, most critics have concentrated on the *impracticality* of seizing oil fields intact. If "armchair strategists still maintain that Saudi Arabia's oil fields can be seized by the U.S. with relative ease," *Newsweek* senior editor Arnaud de Borchgrave wrote after visiting the oil fields in 1975, "they are wrong." Some 700 wells, he noted, are scattered over an area the size of Western Europe; these wells are connected by 7,000 miles of pipeline—most of it aboveground—to 150 processing plants and pumping stations. These facilities, if destroyed by sabotage, "would take years—not months—to put in order." In the final analysis, de Borchgrave asserted, "Intervention would precipitate the very event it is supposed to prevent: the economic strangulation of Western industrialized society."[27]

This conclusion was backed by a more recent study conducted by the Congressional Research Service (CRS) of the Library of Congress. The CRS study, by John M. Collins and Mark R. Clyde, was undertaken at the request 43 of Congressional leaders who wanted to know if America has the *military capacity* to seize and operate Saudi oil fields in response to an embargo or other cutoff in production. After reviewing the problems cited by de Borchgrave, they concluded that even in the "best case" scenario (i.e., no Soviet involvement), U.S. forces would be inadequate to seize and protect all the critical installations involved. "Military forces needed to seize and secure a lodgment on Persian Gulf shores could cope with cratered airfield runways and ruined port facilities, but could neither restore petroleum installations nor operate the system." Saboteurs, meanwhile, "could impede, or perhaps even stop, the flow of oil at its source in the fields, at pipeline choke points, at terminal facilities, or after products have been pumped aboard tankers."[28]

Such studies, widely reported in the military press, have acted as an inhibition on the further elaboration of intervention schemes. But the impulse to "seize Arab oil" remains strong, and there are plenty of studies showing that de Borchgrave, Collins, and Marks have underestimated America's capacity for overcoming these impediments. It is essential, therefore, that we go beyond the issue of efficacy to ask if there are *other reasons* for opposing intervention in the Gulf area.

Calculating the Risks and Benefits

First, even if an oil intervention were successful, *would it justify all the risks and costs involved?* Let's assume that U.S. forces capture Saudi oil installations intact and that sufficient U.S. personnel are available to replace Arab oil workers. Even if other hostile powers (the U.S.S.R., Iraq, Syria) are deterred from an immediate challenge to a U.S. takeover, our military problems would just begin. To protect some 700 wells and 7,000 miles of vulnerable pipeline against sabotage would require a permanent occupation force of several divisions—perhaps 100,000 or more men—who would have to be supplied from bases thousands of miles away in the Pacific and Atlantic. (Just providing *drinking water* for such a force would prove a Herculean and perhaps an impossible task.) Furthermore, tankers traveling to distant ports would have to be escorted through minefields in the Strait of Hormuz and Arabian Sea, and would require continuous protection against terrorist attacks elsewhere. All this would require an effort comparable (in money and manpower) to the U.S. involvment in Vietnam.[29]

And that would be just the beginning: every Arab nation, of whatever ideological orientation, would be forced to counter the U.S. action with an embargo on remaining oil supplies, through economic warfare (by dumping surplus "petrodollars" on the world's monetary markets), and by possible military action against U.S. assets and allies elsewhere. To protect all these interests would require a mobilization of forces unlike anything seen since World War II. Front-line units would have to be withdrawn from Europe, Japan, Korea, and other strategic locales to fill the immedidate manpower need, thus exposing the United States to attacks elsewhere. At some point, we might be forced to use nuclear weapons in defense of one or another besieged outpost or ally, thus risking a global nuclear conflagration. And *no one could predict the duration of such clashes*: strikes, sabotage, terrorism, hit-and-run attacks, and guerrilla warfare could continue for years, sapping our economy and alienating our allies.

Any reckoning of long-term risks and costs, moreover, would have to consider the impact of such action on American society. Instead of promoting traditional U.S. values of cooperation and friendship with others, former Deputy Assistant Secretary of State James H. Noyes said recently, "the interventionists would take us back to an imperial era in which the U.S. would act not so much as the world's policeman, but as its imperial czar, dispatching expeditionary forces to secure strategic natural resources or waterways whenever the natives misused their limited powers."[30] Such a stance might have appeal for swashbucklers like Tucker and Ignotus, but it would prove increasingly distasteful to most Americans—especially if, as is altogether likely, Washington found it necessary to reinstate the draft in order to obtain sufficient "grunts" for such an intervention. As the conflict dragged on, moreover, no American would be altogether exempt from the burdens of war: taxes would go up, living standards would deteriorate, the cities would decay at an even faster rate, key industries would collapse for lack of foreign trade, and—

45

the final blow—oil would be as scarce as ever because the military would consume whatever surplus supplies were pumped out of captured Middle Eastern wells.

Finally, we must ask: *is there an alternative?* In practice, this critical question breaks down into two interrelated issues: first, can we retain access to Mideast oil without going to war?; and second, can we survive *without* Mideast oil? Most U.S. strategists believe that we can be assured of Mideast oil *only* if we're prepared to fight for it. That, in essence, is the rationale for the Carter Doctrine. Strangely, however, neither Western Europe nor Japan—both of which are far more dependent on Mideast oil than we are—have ever felt compelled to adopt a 'Carter Doctrine' of their own. Because OPEC countries *must sell oil* in order to gain the technology they seek, and because *only* the industrialized West can provide both the markets and the technology required by the oil producers, most European and Japanese strategists believe that the Gulf countries will take whatever steps are necessary to assure continued oil deliveries. To be sure, some military aid and technical assistance is required to enable local officials to maintain stability, but the presence of outside forces, in their view, merely complicates the security problem.[31]

But what about the Russians? And what about the risk of another oil embargo? Many strategists believe that Moscow can be deterred from invading the Gulf by U.S. threats to foment trouble in other locales—e.g., Eastern Europe or the Far East—where the Russians are far more vulnerable. (Indeed, former Defense Secretary Brown suggested as much when he told the Council on Foreign Relations in 1980 that any future conflict between American and Soviet forces" over Mideast oil "carries the risk of intensification and geographical spread of the conflict."[32]) Likewise, most analysts believe that OPEC's prosperity has become far too dependent on Western economic stability for Arab leaders to risk their own demise by shutting off oil. Such arguments do not, of course, guarantee that the worst will not come to pass. On the other hand, advocates of U.S. military action cannot promise uninterrupted access to Mideast oil, either. At best, such action would assure partial deliveries at the cost of a permanent military presence; at worst it would produce a global recession and possibly a new world war. On balance, therefore, it would

"Would it not be better to set about to eliminate, by a really serious and determined effort, a dependence [on Persian Gulf oil] that ought never have been allowed to arise, than to try to shore up by military means, in a highly unfavorable region, the unsound position into which the dependence has led us?"

—George Kennan,
The New York Times,
February 1, 1980.

appear that going to war is not necessarily the best way to assure continued petroleum supplies from the Gulf area.

Ultimately, the surest way to overcome any threat to our "vital interest" in the Persian Gulf is to reduce our dependence on imported oil. Many experts believe that a determined conservation effort and alternative supply programs—using solar, wind, and geothermal energy sources—could eliminate the U.S. "dependence" on Middle Eastern oil entirely.

Reducing our Mideast oil imports will not, of course, prove all that easy. The development of synthetic fuels and other alternative supplies is likely to be far more expensive than continued reliance on Persian Gulf crude. On the other hand, any war for Mideast oil is likely to be far more costly than the development of new energy supplies. Start-up costs for the Rapid Deployment Force alone are estimated at $20-25 billion, and a new "Fifth Fleet" for deployment in the Indian Ocean will probably cost twice as much. And those are *peacetime* costs; any full-scale "energy war" in the Gulf area will probably cost several times the $250 billion spent on the Vietnam War (which was fought, after all, with cheap, pre-OPEC gasoline). When we add the potential cost in human lives, and the risk of nuclear escalation, it is obvious that converting to non-Mideast energy sources would be the most economical and prudent solution by far.

In pursuing a non-interventionist posture, it is worth remembering that our dependence on Middle Eastern oil is a relatively *new phenomenon*. Until very recently, the United States managed almost exclusively with Western Hemisphere (USA, Canada, Venezuela) supplies, and it is only because soaring demand outpaced available production that we had to turn eastward. It follows, therefore, that if we can hold down consumption through conservation, and work out an equitable trade relationship with Canada and Mexico, we can gradually reduce our dependence on Mideast oil and thus diminish the risk of a catastrophic energy war. As former diplomat George F. Kennan has observed, "Would it not be better to set about to eliminate, by a really serious and determined effort, a dependence that ought never have been allowed to arise, than to try to shore up by military means, in a highly unfavorable region, the unsound position into which the dependence has led us?"[33]

IV:
THE HAIG DOCTRINE:
GUARDING SCARCE
MINERALS

In the late 1970s, just as the American public was beginning
to cope with the energy crisis, U.S. strategists began warning of *another* materials crisis that they believe may prove
even more threatening: U.S. dependence on imported supplies of critical minerals. Although the United States is
largely self-sufficient in most basic metals (including iron,
copper, and lead), it must import certain other minerals—
chromium, manganese, cobalt, platinum, columbium, and
others less familiar—which are not found or not produced
in this country. Because these materials are absolutely
essential for the production of many high-technology products (especially military products), and because many of
them are found in turbulent Third World areas far from
U.S. shores, a growing number of U.S. policymakers believe that we must use military force if necessary to protect
key sources of scarce minerals—just as, under the Carter
Doctrine, we are now pledged to use force in the protection
of critical oil supplies.[1]

Concern over strategic materials is not, of course, an
entirely new phenomenon. In the early Cold War period,
for instance, U.S. strategists often talked of a Soviet threat
to free world mineral supplies when advocating a policy of
"Containment," and protection of Malayan tin and rubber
was later cited as a rationale for U.S. involvement in the
Indochina conflict. After Vietnam, however, the minerals
issue was largely forgotten until the Arab oil embargo again
raised the question of U.S. dependence on imported raw
materials. At first, this discussion focused exclusively on
the problem of energy supplies, but eventually the minerals

49

issue re-emerged with surprising intensity. In a special issue entitled "Now the Squeeze on Metals," *Business Week* warned in 1979 that "growing U.S. dependence on foreign supplies [of critical minerals] . . . amounts to a strategic threat every bit as damaging as the energy squeeze."[2] A year later, the American Geological Institute carried this alarmist theme one step further when it reported that "All of the oil in the world is of no value if the engines and machines to use it cannot be built or maintained. Without manganese, chromium, platinum and cobalt there can be no automobiles, no airplanes, no jet engines, no satellites, and no sophisticated weapons."[3]

As a result of such exposure, the minerals-dependency problem has recently become a major political issue. Ronald Reagan attacked President Carter for his vacillation on this issue during the 1980 campaign, and other U.S. leaders have taken to raising the topic while addressing larger questions of foreign policy. But, while many politicians have jumped on the minerals bandwagon, none has done so with as much enthusiasm and vigor as Secretary of State Alexander Haig. "I have long been troubled," he told the House Mining Subcommittee in September 1981, "by what is rapidly becoming a crisis in strategic and critical materials." Not only is the United States "inordinately and increasingly dependent on foreign sources of supply," but we must also compete with the Soviet Union for influence and control over many key producing areas in Asia, Africa, and Latin America. "As one assesses the recent step-up of Soviet proxy activities in the Third World," he averred, "then one can only conclude that *the era of the 'resource war' has arrived.*"[4] (Emphasis added.)

These remarks, made while Haig was president of the United Technologies Corp. (UTC), attracted considerable publicity and helped boost his image as an important public figure. Shortly thereafter, Haig's name began appearing regularly in association with that of Ronald Reagan—who now also began hammering away at the minerals issue. Following the election, Reagan appointed a Haig associate from UTC, John M. Oblak, as head of a special task force on strategic materials,[5] and then, to the consternation of many, chose Haig as Secretary of State.

Although, since taking office, Haig has devoted most of his attention to attacks on the Soviet Union and Cuba, he

"Disruption from abroad threatens a more vulnerable West as we draw energy and raw materials from regions in which the throes of rapid change and conflict prevail."

—Secretary of State Alexander Haig,
Washington, April 26, 1981.

has not neglected the materials issue. In a March 1981 interview with the editors of *Time* magazine, he warned that increasing "lawlessness and terrorism" in the Third World are jeopardizing our ability to "assure access to raw materials." Several weeks later, he told the American Society of Newspaper Editors that "Disruption from abroad threatens a more vulnerable West as we draw energy and raw materials from regions in which the throes of rapid change and conflict prevail."[6] In line with these warnings, Haig has consistently argued that the United States must use force if necessary to protect overseas sources of critical materials. Because this stance is likely to enjoy more and more favor in the years ahead, and because the Secretary of State is indisputably the most conspicuous proponent of this policy, it is appropriate that we describe the military solution to America's minerals dependency as the "Haig Doctrine."

As is readily apparent, the Haig Doctrine is a natural extension of and complement to the more familiar "Carter Doctrine." Both doctrines are predicated on a relentless need for imported materials—Carter's for oil and Haig's for minerals—and both rely ultimately on military force to assure U.S. access to such materials when threatened by conflict or disorder abroad. Both, moreover, are fully consistent with the "econocentric" military posture first proposed by former Secretary of Defense Harold Brown (and thus described by some analysts as the "Brown Doctrine"). Because U.S. economic interests in the Third World are threatened by growing "turbulence,"—Brown argued,—we must take military action when necessary to protect these critical assets.[7] (see Chapter II.)

The Haig Doctrine is a natural outgrowth of Brown's position, but also contains some special features which make it   51 especially attractive to the proponents of an interventionist military posture. First of all, the public is already persuaded of the need to protect imported petroleum, and so should be primed to support any steps taken in defense of imported minerals. Second, mineral deposits are scattered all over the face of the globe, and thus a minerals-oriented posture would require an even bigger expansion of military capabilities than that required for protection of imported oil. (The Pentagon has estimated that it will cost $5-$10 billion per year to guard Persian Gulf oil supplies,[8] so it is reasonable to conclude that defense of key mineral supplies in Africa, Asia, and Latin America could add another $10-$15 billion to the Pentagon budget.) Finally, as more and more Americans become convinced that raw materials shortages will produce a measurable decline in their standard of living, the base of popular support for an activist military posture will presumably grow accordingly.

Given the perceived benefits of a minerals-oriented defense policy, it is hardly surprising that all four military services have joined the hue and cry over imported materials. None, however, has pursued this issue with more determination than the U.S. Navy. In a 1978 pamphlet entitled *U.S. Life Lines*, the Navy Department argued that imported raw materials are essential "to the operation of the vast U.S. industrial machine with its millions of wage earners," and that therefore any disruption in those supplies would severely impair our capacity "to achieve our national objectives in time of war and to support our way of life in time of peace."[9]

This outlook, assiduously cultivated by the Navy Department over the past few years, has won numerous converts in Washington and begun to pay handsome dividends. In both 1979 and 1980, Congress voted to procure more ships than the Carter Administration thought necessary, and in 1981 the Reagan Administration committed itself to a massive expansion of U.S. naval strength. These moves have been accompanied, moreover, by formal recognition of the Haig Doctrine and adoption of the more vigorous military policy it implies. Because these steps will have profound consequences for U.S. foreign policy—leading, perhaps, to U.S. involvement in a series of bloody "resource wars"—it is essential that we examine the minerals situation closely and its implications for U.S. foreign and military policy.

The "Squeeze on Metals"— How Tight?

While talk of a "squeeze on metals" suggests an America largely dependent on foreign supplies, in reality the United States is relatively well endowed with mineral resources. According to *Business Week*, America consumes about $140 billion worth of metals per year (in 1979 dollars), of which only $10 billion, or 7 percent, is imported.[10] For most of the basic metals, including iron ore, copper, and lead, U.S. sources provide most or all domestic requirements and even, in some cases, a surplus for export. The United States also has very large reserves of other minerals— including cobalt, platinum, titanium, and chromium— which are not presently mined here for economical or environmental reasons, but which could be exploited if foreign sources were cut off.[11]

Despite this generally rosy picture, however, the United States must turn to foreign sources for some critical materials not found or not currently produced in this country. Among the minerals most often listed in this strategic category are: columbium, titanium (rutile), manganese, cobalt, bauxite, chromium, tin, nickel, and zinc. U.S. dependency on foreign sources of these materials range from 90-100 percent for the first six to 81 percent for tin, 77 percent for nickel, and 62 percent for zinc.[12] These materials, and others even more obscure, are not always consumed in great quantity; but because they are used to produce high-strength alloys and other substances used in modern industry, are considered essential to American economic survival.* Many are also used to produce ad-

---

*Columbium is used to produce fatigue-resistant alloys used in jet engines, refinery equipment, and nuclear reactors; *titanium* is used to produce lightweight alloys for jet aircraft and missiles; *manganese* is a basic building block in the manufacture of steel; *cobalt* is used to produce high-strength, heat-resistant alloys used in jet engines; *bauxite* is the principal ore used to make aluminum; *chromium* and *nickel* are used to make stainless steel and other specialized alloys; *platinum* is used to make catalytic converters in automobiles and as a catalyst in oil refining; *zinc* is used in a wide variety of industrial applications.

> *"Should we become isolated from the rest of the world and our stockpile of raw materials become depleted, the consequences would be severe indeed. The operations of our basic industries would be sharply curtailed for lack of critical materials. In turn there would be a reduction in our capacity to manufacture equipment, including ships, aircraft, and electronics products, all so essential to our national posture."*
>
> —Department of the Navy,
> *U.S. Life Lines.*

vanced military hardware—titanium, for instance, is widely used in the manufacture of supersonic aircraft—and thus are considered essential to national security as well. Without these materials, the Navy warned in 1978, "the sophisticated industrial complexes that provide our high standard of living and superior naval and military ordnance would not be possible."[13]

Fortunately, many of the most essential materials not available here are found in Australia, Canada, Mexico, Brazil, and other countries with close ties to the United States. Canada, for instance, is a major source of colombium, nickel, and zinc, while Australia provides much of our aluminum and titanium ores.[14] But some critical materials are only produced in remote Third World areas where conflict or disorder could threaten U.S. supplies for varying periods of time. War-torn Zaire, for instance, supplies 34 percent of America's cobalt needs, while Malaysia provides 43 percent of our tin and Jamaica 50 percent of our bauxite.[15] Because these and other resource-rich countries "either are, or have the potential of being politically unstable," minerologist David Kroft wrote in *Air Force* magazine, "neither the United States nor its allies can be assured of the long-term availability of minerals from these nations."[16]

54

U.S. IMPORTS OF SELECTED MATERIALS

Mineral	Percentage of U.S. consumption provided by imports	Major sources
Columbium	100	Brazil
Strontium	100	Mexico
Industrial diamonds	100	Ireland, South Africa
Manganese	98	South Africa, France, Japan
Tantalum	96	Thailand, Canada, Malaysia
Bauxite	93	Jamaica, Guinea, Surinam
Cobalt	90	Zaire, Belgium, Zambia
Chromium	90	South Africa, Philippines, Soviet Union
Platinum group	89	South Africa, Soviet Union
Asbestos	85	Canada
Tin	81	Malaysia, Thailand, Indonesia
Nickel	77	Canada
Cadmium	66	Canada, Australia, Mexico
Zinc	62	Canada
Mercury	62	Algeria, Spain, Italy
Tungsten	59	Canada, Bolivia, South Korea
Selenium	40	Canada, Japan, Yugoslavia

Sources: U.S. Bureau of Mines, Sinclair Group Cos.

U.S. strategists are also worried that American dependency on foreign sources is growing. Taking a list of 25 unindentified imported materials, the Joint Chiefs of Staff (JCS) found that "in 1960, our dependency averaged 54 percent," whereas in 1980, "our dependency for the same items averages 70 percent."[17] But while such statements suggest an absolute decline in U.S. minerals supplies, the fact is that the shift towards foreign sources is caused more by the declining profitability of U.S. mines (when compared to overseas supplies which can often be mined at less cost) than by any decline in U.S. reserves.[18] Talking of titanium, for instance, *Fortune* magazine noted in 1981 that "here, the U.S. is dependent on imports by choice. It has abundant reserves of a low-grade ore called ilmenite [but] all titanium produced in this country is made from [imported supplies] of a high-grade ore called rutile because the process is simpler and creates less waste."[19] It follows from this, of course, that the United States can again rely on domestic sources for many materials if foreign supplies are no longer available.

Some materials, however, are just not available in this country. It is for this reason that some analysts believe that the minerals crisis is as threatening as the energy crisis. "The United States is a have-not nation when it comes to certain critical materials," UTC chairman Harry Gray (another Haig associate) observed in 1979. "From 1950 to the present, our raw materials situation has deteriorated drastically," to the point where "today we are frighteningly vulnerable to overseas producers."[20] Not only must we worry about conflict and instability in many key producing areas, but also about possible Soviet efforts to seize control of these supplies. Some observers, including Haig, believe that the Soviets have a long-term plan to overwhelm the "resource lines of the Western world,"[21] but other analysts are skeptical of such a strategy, suggesting only (to quote *Fortune*) that "the Russians are now gaining footholds in Third World countries where they could one day threaten Western access to strategic materials."[22] While there is no doubt that the U.S.S.R. has acquired more influence in Africa and other mineral-rich areas of the Third World, it has not, as yet, made any direct moves to obstruct Western access to overseas suppliers (although, on occasion, the Soviets have attempted to manipulate world prices of certain materials using traditional, "capitalistic" methods in order to increase the value of their own minerals exports). Furthermore, most experts believe that Moscow will continue to refrain from such moves in the future, both from fear of conflict with the West and because, as a major producer itself, it has a vested interest in the stability of world markets.[23] Nevertheless, fears of a Soviet "master plan" persist, and will surely give added credibility to the Haig doctrine in the years ahead.

For those who fear a Soviet or insurgent threat to Western minerals supplies, no area is of greater concern than sub-Saharan Africa. This region, encompassing some of the most prolific concentrations of minerals in the world, now supplies much of the West's cobalt, manganese, chromium, and platinum. Long troubled by racial, political, and tribal unrest, the area is now expected to experience a fresh outbreak of insurgent conflict—accompanied, perhaps, by direct confrontation between the superpowers and their allies and proxies.[24] According to Secretary Haig, the outcome of such fighting will have profound consequences for the West: "Should future trends . . . result in alignment with Moscow of this critical resource area, the U.S.S.R. would control as much as 90 percent of several key minerals for which no substitutes have been developed and the loss of which could bring the severest consequences to the existing economic and security framework of the free world." Given such high stakes, he told the House Mining Subcommittee in 1980, the United States must lobby within NATO for an expanded security policy that would permit joint action to safeguard key minerals supplies in this region.[25]

In the case of South Africa—source of 68 percent of our chromium and 73 percent of our platinum—any such moves would almost automatically involve greater support for the existing, all-white regime in Pretoria, and thus would be vigorously opposed by black states in the area as well as by opponents of *apartheid* in this country. Nevertheless, in homage to the Haig Doctrine, the new Administration appears to be headed towards just such an accommodation. In a television interview with Walter Cronkite on March 3, 1981, President Reagan openly suggested that we cannot "abandon a country that . . . strategically is essential to the free world in its production of minerals that we all must have."[26] Critics of *apartheid* argue, however, that the United States can satisfy its mineral needs without forming an alliance with Pretoria. They argue, for instance, that South Africa will continue selling us minerals no matter what our political stance, for the simple reason that it must have foreign earnings in order to survive economically.[27] Furthermore, if Pretoria cuts back its supplies (say, in retaliation for U.N. sanctions), or if internal chaos results in production cutbacks, we can compensate for any shortfalls by exploiting lower-grade reserves in the United States, by developing alternative supplies in other countries, and through conservation and the re-use of scrap and waste materials.[28] By aligning with the all-white regime in Pretoria, moreover, we run the risk of alienating many black countries in Africa which are also major suppliers of raw materials. As noted by Richard Barnet of the Institute for Policy Studies in *The Lean Years*, "The more the U.S. identifies with the wrong side in South Africa—wrong morally and wrong politically because eventually the white minority will lose—the more it will cut itself off from the majority of nations and peoples on whom it must increasingly depend."[29]

In many ways, the South African situation crystallizes the whole debate on imported strategic materials. Either we can reduce our dependency on any single source through conservation and the development of alternative supplies, or, in line with the Haig Doctrine, we can begin using military force to ensure access to existing supplies. Both solutions will be costly: the development of alternative supplies will require extensive investment in new mines, smelters, and transportation facilities; a military approach will require extensive investment in new warships, combat forces, and overseas basing facilities. But while the costs of the former can be roughly calculated, no one can predict what a minimally-effective military solution might cost—especially if, as is highly possible, U.S. forces get drawn into an extended "resource war" in the Third World. Because the American public is being asked to assume financial responsibility for a military response—however costly—and because such an approach could easily result in a major conflagration, it is essential that we compare the costs and benefits of these two solutions more closely. Before turning to this discussion, however, it is useful to show how a military approach will affect just one of the military services: the United States Navy.

The Navy Makes a Comeback

For most of the past two centuries, the Navy was America's premier military service and the leading recipient of federal expenditures. In the Nuclear Age, however, the Navy surrendered its favored status to the Air Force—which alone of the services can drop "the bomb" on Moscow—while the Army used its NATO responsibilities to move into second place. At one point, some strategists questioned if we even *needed* a Navy, save as an escort service for convoys carrying supplies to allied forces in Europe. But now, as a result of the energy crisis and growing U.S. dependence on imported minerals, the Navy has acquired new prominence as guardian of the world's major sea lanes.

The Navy has been gaining ground since 1974, when the Arab oil embargo dramatized the U.S. dependency on imported raw materials and underscored the strategic significance of the Persian Gulf area. Then, with the fall of the Shah five years later, the United States was left without a reliable ally in this critical region and thus Washington was forced to assume direct responsibility for protection of Mideast oil. When Soviet troops invaded nearby Afghanistan in January 1980, President Carter made explicit what had long been implicit in U.S. policy: that an assault on Persian Gulf oil supplies "will be repelled by any means necessary, including military force."[30] (See Chapter III.) And because the Navy, alone of the military services, has the forces-in-being to conduct sustained military operations in the Gulf area, it was able to assume primary responsibility for enforcement of the "Carter Doctrine."

Flushed with success over its capturing of responsibility for the protection of imported oil, the Navy has mapped out plans for an even more ambitious role as guardian of U.S. minerals imports. Because "these raw materials are globally dispersed," the service noted recently, "they must come to us via the sea." This, in turn, requires an "assurance that sea lanes will be kept open and secure for our commerce"—an assurance that the Navy alone can provide.[31] To prove its point, the Office of the Chief of Naval Operations (CNO) published a study of U.S. minerals imports replete with maps showing the extended sea routes these materials had to traverse before reaching the United States. "These sea lanes," the CNO report noted, "are the Life Lines of America," and their protection "is a vital role of the United States Navy."[32]

This argument has clearly made a strong impression on political leaders of both parties. "We should constantly keep in mind that we are an island nation," Sen. Gary Hart (D.-Colo.) affirmed in a 1979 interview. Because so many "of the raw materials necessary for the fueling of our industrial base" come by sea from distant Third World areas, it is essential that we have "a Navy capable of protecting the sea lanes that carry those raw materials."[33]

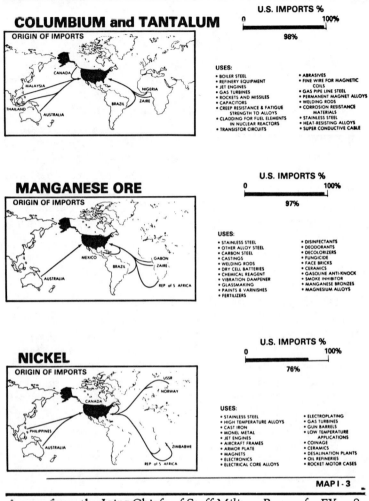

COLUMBIUM and TANTALUM

U.S. IMPORTS %
0   100%
98%

ORIGIN OF IMPORTS

USES:
- BOILER STEEL
- REFINERY EQUIPMENT
- JET ENGINES
- GAS TURBINES
- ROCKETS AND MISSILES
- CAPACITORS
- CREEP RESISTANCE & FATIGUE STRENGTH TO ALLOYS
- CLADDING FOR FUEL ELEMENTS IN NUCLEAR REACTORS
- TRANSISTOR CIRCUITS
- ABRASIVES
- FINE WIRE FOR MAGNETIC COILS
- GAS PIPE LINE STEEL
- PERMANENT MAGNET ALLOYS
- WELDING RODS
- CORROSION RESISTANCE MATERIALS
- STAINLESS STEEL
- HEAT-RESISTING ALLOYS
- SUPER CONDUCTIVE CABLE

MANGANESE ORE

U.S. IMPORTS %
0   100%
97%

ORIGIN OF IMPORTS

USES:
- STAINLESS STEEL
- OTHER ALLOY STEEL
- CARBON STEEL
- CASTINGS
- WELDING RODS
- DRY CELL BATTERIES
- CHEMICAL REAGENT
- VIBRATION DAMPENER
- GLASSMAKING
- PAINTS & VARNISHES
- FERTILIZERS
- DISINFECTANTS
- DEODORANTS
- DECOLORIZERS
- FUNGICIDE
- FACE BRICKS
- CERAMICS
- GASOLINE ANTI-KNOCK
- SMOKE INHIBITOR
- MANGANESE BRONZES
- MAGNESIUM ALLOYS

NICKEL

U.S. IMPORTS %
0   100%
76%

ORIGIN OF IMPORTS

USES:
- STAINLESS STEEL
- HIGH TEMPERATURE ALLOYS
- CAST IRON
- MONEL METAL
- JET ENGINES
- AIRCRAFT FRAMES
- ARMOR PLATE
- MAGNETS
- ELECTRONICS
- ELECTRICAL CORE ALLOYS
- ELECTROPLATING
- GAS TURBINES
- GUN BARRELS
- LOW TEMPERATURE APPLICATIONS
- COINAGE
- CERAMICS
- DESALINATION PLANTS
- OIL REFINERIES
- ROCKET MOTOR CASES

MAP I - 3

A page from the Joint Chiefs of Staff *Military Posture for FY 1982*.

Many Republicans have expressed similar sentiments, and have joined with Democrats in demanding a rapid buildup of naval capabilities. Indeed, so adamant has Congress been on this issue that it repeatedly authorized construction of more ships than the Carter Administration considered necessary. Thus, when Secretary Brown requested $6 billion in 1979 to build 15 new warships in the next fiscal year, Congress appropriated an extra few billion to procure four additional ships (two attack submarines and two FFG-7 guided-missile frigates) and to acquire four *Spruance*-class destroyers originally built for Iran and later cancelled by the new Islamic regime.[34] One year later, when Brown came back with a plan for 17 new ships in Fiscal 1981, Congress again proposed construction of still another four ships (two submarines and two FFG-7s). Had Mr. Carter been re-elected President in 1980, he would almost certainly have faced yet another fight in Congress over the Navy's shipbuilding program; with Mr. Reagan in the White House, however, such contests have become a thing of the past.

Not since World War II has the Navy found a patron as forthcoming as Ronald Reagan. During the campaign, Mr. Reagan attacked President Carter for "dismantling U.S. Naval and Marine Forces," and pledged to "restore our fleet to 600 ships" from its present level of 450.[35] Once in office, he moved quickly to implement this pledge: the Navy's shipbuilding allocation for Fiscal 1981-82 was increased by 57 percent, from $6.6 billion under the Carter plan to $10.5 billion in the revised budget—making the Navy the number one recipient of Pentagon funds in the process. These additional billions will be used to begin construction on a new nuclear-powered aircraft carrier, and to procure one additional CG-47 missile cruiser, two more FFG-7s, one submarine, and six more SL-7 container ships for the Rapid Deployment Force. In addition, Mr. Reagan proposed reactivating two World War II-vintage battleships, the *Iowa* and the *New Jersey*, along with the aircraft carrier *Oriskany*. And this is only the first step in the Administration's ambitious naval program: over the next five years, Reagan will add an estimated $150 billion to the Defense budget in order to bring U.S. naval strength up to the 600-ship level promised during the campaign, and to create a new "Fifth Fleet" for permanent service in the Indian Ocean area.[36]

Many factors are involved in the Reagan Administration's determination to expand U.S. naval capabilities—including traditional commitments to NATO and the growth of Soviet naval forces—but concern over imported raw materials clearly remains the dominant motive. In justifying the Administration's proposal to add $3.8 billion to the Navy's shipbuilding account in Fiscal 1982, Defense Secretary Caspar Weinberger told Congress that "We are, in a very real sense, an island nation. American commerce and industry, access to vital resources, and the sinews of the Western Alliance depend on our ability to control the seas. We must be able to defeat any military adversary who threatens such access."[37] The same theme was echoed by JCS Chairman Gen. David C. Jones in his Fiscal 1982 report on U.S. Military Posture: "The world's oceans are still vital as a commercial bridge across which travel many of the raw materials, minerals, trade goods, and energy supplies needed to sustain a vigorous U.S. economy."[38] Given this concurrence, and given the proven support of Congress, it is obvious that the Navy will prosper in the years ahead. And if this year's budget is any indication, it will soon regain its historical role as America's premier military service.

Unrestrained military spending, coupled with unlimited political backing, can obviously produce a fleet big enough to defeat any potential adversary at sea. For some, this is an appropriate response to the problem of U.S. dependence on imported raw materials; but neither Mr. Weinberger nor Mr. Haig, nor any of the other proponents of a military response, have yet explained how a bigger Navy will assure the flow of minerals if supplying countries are torn apart by regional conflict or civil unrest. True, we can send in the Marines—but how many? And for how long? And to what end? These questions, as yet unanswered, must be addressed if we are to develop a sane and effective response to the minerals problem.

Finding a Solution— Are "Resource Wars" the Only Answer?

Although the Haig Doctrine has not yet replaced the Carter Doctrine as the driving force behind U.S. military policy in the Third World, it should be apparent, from all we have learned here, that the minerals issue is gaining momentum and will undoubtedly have a major impact in the years ahead. Already, as shown above, it has sparked a major expansion in U.S. naval capabilities and a shift in U.S. policy towards South Africa. Further consequences—

including a growing likelihood of U.S. intervention in mineral-rich areas—are sure to follow.

The most immediate effect of these developments on U.S. society will, of course, be increased military expenditures. Reagan's plan to enlarge the Navy from 450 to 600 warships will cost an estimated $120 billion. (A new aircraft carrier task group, including accompanying aircraft and escort vessels, costs some $10-12 billion alone—and Reagan wants to add two of these for the proposed "Fifth Fleet" in the Indian Ocean.) Formation of the Rapid Deployment Force (RDF) will cost another $20-$25 billion, and new overseas basing facilities could add $5-$10 billion more. And all this is just for fixed assets; operating costs of the new ships and forces, if deployed on a continuing basis in remote Third World areas, could cost an additional $10 to $15 billion per year. And then there's the question of conscription: many experts doubt that the Armed Services can attract all the extra recruits it will need to staff these new forces through the existing, all-volunteer system, and thus it is likely that U.S. leaders will press for early reinstatement of the draft.

For proponents of a military response to the minerals problem, none of this is too high a price to pay for assured supplies of critical materials. But there is yet another factor that must be introduced into the equation: the risk of war. History suggests than an increased U.S. military presence in volatile Third World areas—coupled with a policy of using military force to protect key minerals supplies—will automatically increase the risk of U.S. involvement in a protracted "resource war." Such a war could prove extraordinarily expensive—with gasoline now costing $1.50 per gallon, any replay of Vietnam (fought with oil costing 25¢ per gallon) would cost $1 trillion or more—and produce great human suffering. And even if U.S. forces triumphed on the battlefield, they could not guarantee the resumption of minerals production—especially if, as is only all too likely—the original workforce is dead or in hiding.

Because the costs of a military solution are so great, and because it could easily result in a series of crippling "resource wars," it behooves us to ask if there is an alternative solution to the problem of scarce materials. After examining all the factors involved, and assuming continued progress in materials research, the answer is a very firm *yes*.

Looked at objectively, the U.S. minerals situation is just not as precarious as the alarmists would have us believe. To begin with, the United States has a "national defense stockpile" with some $13.5 billion worth of critical materials stored away for some future catastrophe.* If brought up to target levels for all 62 materials involved—an effort that will cost an estimated $6 billion (far less than Reagan wants to spend *each year* on naval shipbuilding)—the stockpile will provide enough supplies to satisfy *all* U.S. military requirements for three years of combat during a major war, while *simultaneously* providing for essential civilian needs.[41] Furthermore, as noted earlier, the United States has abundant reserves of many critical minerals which are not being mined now because of high costs (high, that is, when compared to the cost of exploiting foreign, higher-grade ores), but which could be used to satisfy many U.S. requirements if foreign supplies were reduced or eliminated. Among the minerals in this category are cobalt, titanium, manganese, platinum, and chromium.[42] Speaking of the latter, the director of the U.S. Bureau of Mines, Dr. John Morgan, noted recently that "Even though U.S. chromium is low grade and costly to mine and produce, it could be used if our import source is cut off." The same is true, he noted, for many of the other metals in the strategic category.[43]

In those cases where no domestic supplies are known to exist, we have other options besides war. First, we can assist *alternative suppliers* in other, friendly countries to expand production at existing mines and to develop new ones. Because any cutback in production at established sources of a given material will automatically raise the world price of that substance, such expansion would be in the direct economic interest of the countries involved and thus re-

---

*Included in the stockpile (as of 1980) are: 41 million pounds of cobalt, 200,000 tons of tin, 20 million carats of industrial diamonds, 32,000 tons of titanium sponge, 1,000 tons of beryllium, 140 million ounces of silver, 1.3 million tons of chromium, 200,000 tons of manganese, and 85 million pounds of tungsten.[39] In March 1981, President Reagan announced that the General Services Administration would sell off some of the tin, tungsten and silver in the stockpile in order to finance purchases of more critical materials, particularly cobalt, bauxite, opium salts (for medicine), nickel, columbium, and titanium. These additions are necessary, Reagan declared, because "our nation is vulnerable to sudden shortages in basic raw materials that are necessary to our production base."[40]

quire little prodding from Washington. Any decline in supplies of South African manganese, for instance, would (according to *The Washington Post*) "encourage a step-up in mining in Australia, India, Brazil, and a number of African countries," while a decline in South African chrome "would make mining in countries like Turkey and the Philippines more profitable."[44] Second, we can develop *substitute materials* using new and ingenious combinations of readily-available substances to duplicate the properties on unobtainable minerals. Such hybrid products use small quantities of precious metals like titanium along with graphite-reinforced alloys to produce a "metal matrix composite" (MMC) every bit as strong as the original metal. Such composites are already being used in the fabrication of U.S. military aircraft and, according to Dr. Arden L. Bemet of the Department of Defense, current research indicates "the potential for substitution of MMC for critical . . . elements such as chromium, cobalt, titanium and beryllium."[45] Finally, we can institute *conservation* measures as in the energy area, and increase the *reclamation* of scrap and waste materials. Consider: a new plant in Ellwood City, Pa., operated by the International Metals Reclamation Corp., will annually convert 50,000 tons of steel mill waste into some 9 million pounds of chromium, 4 million pounds of nickel, 600,000 pounds of molybdenum, and 32 million pounds of iron.[46] Such efforts, combined with a significant program of conservation, could help make up for any short-term decline in imports, and provide time to develop alternative supplies in the United States and elsewhere.

The development of new minerals supplies will not, of course, prove simple or inexpensive. To bring the national stockpile up to desired levels will cost an estimated $6 billion, while construction of new mines and processing facilities could cost several times that amount. It will also be necessary to reconcile the nation's need for minerals and the equally vital need to protect our fast-vanishing wilderness areas. But the United States clearly has the resources and the capabilities to undertake such an effort, and to do so without ravaging the environment. And however costly such and effort may become, it cannot begin to approach the costs of an unlimited naval buildup or a prolonged resource war in the Third World.

Admittedly, the development of new materials and

sources will not, in all cases, assure the United States of full immunity from future cutoffs of critical raw materials. Future upheavals, like the current fighting between Iraq and Iran, may temporarily curtail our access to some minerials. We could, in such cases, invoke the Haig Doctrine and use military force to ensure U.S. access to the disputed materials. But no one has indicated what form such action would take, and how it would guarantee the resumption of deliveries if the local workforce refuses to cooperate with U.S. authorities. And if, instead of fleeing, the local population chooses to resist U.S. intervention, we could find ourselves in an expanding conflagration that would consume far more fuel and materials than would ever reach our shores from that area once the war is won.

It should appear, from all this, that the Haig Doctrine offers no real solution to the problem of scarce mineral supplies. As in the case of our energy needs, the more prudent and economical course would be to lessen our dependency on individual foreign suppliers rather than to permit such dependencies to draw us into a catastrophic— and possibly futile—resource war. And, once we adopt this approach, we will soon discover that the minerals problem is far more manageable than Secretary Haig would have us believe. "As long as we keep up our science and technology," Dr. Morgan observed recently, "the world has more resources now than ever, and there will be even more in the future. Given relative peace in the world, reasonable price incentives, and a continued effort in technological development, *we're not going to run out of anything.*"[47] (Emphasis added.)

V.
THE RAPID DEPLOYMENT FORCE: AN ARMY IN SEARCH OF A WAR

Not since the Green Berets were lionized by President Kennedy in 1961 has a U.S. military unit advanced so far so quickly as the newly-formed Rapid Deployment Force (RDF). In 1979, the RDF was nothing but a rough sketch on the Pentagon's drawing boards; in 1980, it had a name, a commander, a skeleton staff, and nothing else; by 1981, it could boast an elaborate headquarters complex, an incipient basing apparatus in the Middle East, and command jurisdiction over four Army divisions, a Marine Amphibious Force of one division plus associated air wing, three aircraft carrier task groups, dozens of Air Force tactical squadrons, and a supporting cast of several hundred thousand men and women. And, if President Reagan pursues the "more aggressive" military policy his aides have championed, the RDF may soon have the dubious privilege of being the first U.S. force to enter combat since the end of the Vietnam War.

When first conceived in 1977, the RDF was seen as a lean, self-reliant strike force designed for rapid insertion into remote Third World battlefields. As the concept has matured, however, the force has evolved into a full-scale army with a growing transport, logistics, and communications establishment. Once numbered 100,000, the RDF now encompasses some 200,000 soldiers and sailors, and could swell to 300,000 or more if, as expected, Mr. Reagan approves the formation of additional ground combat units.

Along with its growth in size, the RDF has experienced a corresponding increase in responsibilities. Originally, the force was intended to serve as a mobile "fire brigade" for

67

"I would feel comfortable in going to war tomorrow."
—Gen. P.X. Kelley,
Washington, October 1, 1980.

dousing Third World conflicts deemed injurious to U.S. interests. Like the famed 11th Parachute Regiment of France, it was conceived as a lightly-armed strike force that could be airlifted on short notice to overseas hot-spots, overpower the local opposition, and then fly out again before anyone had time to organize protests. But while the force retains a fire-brigade role of this sort, it has also been assigned the far demanding tasks of stopping a hypothetical Soviet invasion of the Persian Gulf and of seizing Saudi oil fields in the event of a regional conflagration. In recognition of these added responsibilities, the RDF is now being elevated to a full-scale joint command (like the existing European Command, Pacific Command, and Southern Command) with operational jurisdiction over the Southwest Asia region. And because any military engagements in this region would probably require a powerful army equipped with tanks and artillery, the RDF has had to incorporate more and more combat units and to develop an elaborate system of supply bases in Egypt, Oman, Kenya and Somalia.

And because even these accretions are not considered adequate for any really demanding contingency, the RDF has adopted a dangerous new "pre-emptive strategy" calling for military intervention *in advance* of anticipated enemy action. The intent of the new policy, RDF commander General Paul X. Kelley explained in 1980, is to ensure that U.S. forces occupy the battlefield *first*, thus signalling to an opponent that any hostile action on its part is likely to trigger a full-scale confrontation with American power. Such pre-emptive action could, according to Kelley, persuade the enemy commander to "bow out gracefully"; it is equally likely, however, that such action would trigger a full-scale military conflict of unforeseeable proportions.

While this prospect should be sufficiently terrifying to give anyone pause for reflection, critics of the existing RDF program have concentrated almost exclusively on the issue of *adequacy*: is the new force adequately armed and prepared to face likely contingencies arising in the Middle East?

68

Although RDF skeptics—including most advisers to President Reagan—maintain that the answer is "no," Pentagon officials insist that the new force is fully capable of protecting U.S. interests abroad. "I would feel comfortable in going to war tomorrow," General Kelley affirmed on October 1, 1980.[1] To prove his point, Kelley has staged a succession of elaborate RDF military exercises in the United States and abroad, including the much-publicized "Operation Bright Star" in Egypt.

Like the Green Berets in the 1960s, the RDF is now seeking a battlefield upon which to demonstrate its capabilities. Given the rush of world events, and the Reagan Administration's evident determination to restore the "credibility" of American power, it is likely that the RDF will soon have its wish. Such an opportunity could arise at almost any moment in the Persian Gulf, North Africa, or any one of a number of hot spots around the globe. Because such an engagement could easily escalate into a major conflagration, and because Pentagon officials talk openly of using tactical nuclear weapons in such a contingency, it is essential that we take a good hard look at the RDF and its governing doctrine. As we shall see, such a survey can also tell us a great deal about the evolution of U.S. foreign policy since Vietnam, and about the risk of global conflict in the 1980s.

The Evolution of the R.D.F.

The concept of a mobile intervention force first materialized in early 1977, when President Carter directed the National Security Council (NSC) to conduct an overview of U.S. military capabilities. The resulting document, Presidential Review Memorandum #10 (PRM-10), warned that the United States was not fully equipped to deal with crises arising in the Third World, and particularly in the oil-rich Persian Gulf area. On the basis of this study, Carter ordered the Department of Defense to organize a mobile strike force for use in non-NATO contingencies. Carter's decree, known as Presidential Directive #18 (PD-18), was never made public; Pentagon correspondents were told, however, that it called for a "special contingent for waging 'brush-fire' wars in the Third World."[2] As originally conceived, this was to be a relatively light force of perhaps 100,000 troops,

69

capable of going anywhere and operating independently of existing bases and logistical facilities.

Although the RDF was not to be heard of again for nearly two years, the decision to undertake its formation clearly represented a major turning-point in U.S. military policy. At the end of the Vietnam War, the U.S. public adopted a "never again" stance on the use of American ground forces in Third World conflicts—the stance we know as the "Vietnam Syndrome." In adjusting to these restraints, U.S. strategists forged a new, "post-Vietnam" military policy stressing support for NATO and other traditional alliances, along with the cultivation of "surrogate gendarmes" like Iran that could be induced (through massive transfusions of U.S. arms) to protect critical Third World areas on Washington's behalf. Theoretically, the emergence of such surrogates would free U.S. ground forces from future "peace-keeping" responsibilities, and thus permit an expanded U.S. commitment to NATO. But many strategists believed that surrogate forces were inherently unreliable, and that an American interventionary force of some sort was needed to protect growing U.S. economic interests in the Third World. Carter's decision to proceed with formation of the RDF suggests, therefore, that while the Administration continued to support the post-Vietnam posture in public, it was already moving in private towards a pre-Vietnam view of military power.[3]

Despite this turnaround in elite thinking, the U.S. public retained its attachment to the Vietnam Syndrome and thus the Administration conducted its RDF deliberations under a shroud of secrecy. At first, work on this force proceeded slowly because of dissension within the Pentagon over which of the four Armed Services was to have jurisdiction over the new command. But then, two events occurred which transformed the entire discussion of military policy: the fall of the Shah, and the global "energy crisis" which followed. The first event erased all remaining confidence in the surrogate model, while the second demonstrated just how dependent the Western economies had become on Persian Gulf oil. As a result, U.S. policymakers repudiated whatever remained of the post-Vietnam posture and reaffirmed the need for an independent U.S. interventionary capability. As noted in Chapter II, the Carter Administration's new stance was unveiled on February 25, 1979, when

Secretary Brown told a nationwide television audience that the United States would "take any action that's appropriate, including the use of military force," to protect oil imports from the Middle East.[4]

With this sort of mandate, planning for the new force moved ahead rapidly. On June 21, 1979, outgoing Army Chief of Staff General Bernard W. Rogers provided reporters with a preliminary look at the proposed command. As then conceived, the unit was to be a "quick-strike force" of about 100,000 men who would be trained and equipped to fight in "the Persian Gulf, Middle East, Northeast Asia," or wherever else there was a contingency outside of NATO.[5] According to Rogers, this unit—then called the "Unilateral Force" because it would be used independently of NATO and other alliance systems—would be built around the 82nd Airborne Division and two other Army divisions.[6]

Before these plans could be implemented, however, the Pentagon was again shaken by a round of inter-service wrangling over the leadership and composition of the proposed force. Some defense planners suggested that most Army units were already committed to NATO or Korea, and that light infantry divisions like the 82nd were not equipped to fight Soviet-style armored forces of the sort found in Syria. Leaders of the Marine Corps, meanwhile, argued that they were not similarly constrained by prior commitments, and that the Marines—with their integral amphibious lift and air-support capabilities—were better equipped for quick-strike missions outside the NATO area.[7] "I think it is pertinent to keep in mind," Navy Chief of Operations Adm. Thomas B. Hayward avowed, "that the Navy-Marine Corps team was this country's original Rapid Deployment Force, going back many years; and that our carrier battle-groups and amphibious forces forward deployed today near potential trouble spots remain the country's most immediately available capability for the application of military power in situations where U.S. interests may require it."[8] Much to the surprise of the Army, this argument found strong backing in Washington and so, when the dust finally settled on the inter-service conflict, the Marines emerged with initial command authority over the quick-strike force.

Planning for the new detachment, now rechristened the

"The vital interests of the United States, Western Europe and Japan in Saudi oilfields would necessitate military action if our interests were threatened. If that required organization of strike forces, there would be strong support for this on Capital Hill."

—Sen. Frank Church, in *The New York Times*, December 2, 1979.

Rapid Deployment Force, was already well advanced by November 1979 when the hostage takeover in Teheran lent fresh urgency to the organizing effort. Reaction to the takeover was particularly intense in Congress, where many lawmakers called for a rapid expansion of U.S. interventionary capabilities.[9] The hostage crisis also intensified Congressional concern over Mideast oil supplies, leading Sen. Franch Church of Idaho to declare that if protection of the oil flow "required organization of strike forces," there would be "strong support for this on Capital Hill."[10]

In response to Congressional prodding for quick action on the RDF program, Pentagon officials finally went public with their emerging plans on December 5, 1979. At a press briefing in the Pentagon, General Kelley of the Marine Corps—soon to be named RDF commander—provided the first detailed picture of RDF structure and doctrine. The new command would not have any permanently-assigned forces of its own, he explained, but rather would have "drawdown" authority over selected Army, Navy, Marine, and Air Force units which would fall under RDF authority in the event of war. These units, which were to include the Army's 82nd and 101st Airborne Divisions plus three Marine amphibious brigades, would constitute a "reservoir" of U.S.-based troops which would be assembled in various "force packages" depending on the contingency at hand (see box on RDF components). At the outbreak of a crisis, these selected units would be flown to bases in friendly countries near the conflict area, where they would pick up their heavy equipment from supply ships that had been "prepositioned" in adjacent waters. Once "married

72

R.D.F. Components

As presently organized, the Rapid Deployment Force does not have any permanently-assigned forces of its own, but rather has a headquarters staff—the Rapid Deployment Joint Task Force (RDJTF) at MacDill Air Force Base, Florida—which has "draw down" rights over selected Army, Navy, Marine, and Air Force units. These units constitute a "reservoir" of combat forces which can be assembled by the RDJTF into various "force packages" depending on the contingency involved. Among the units which are available for assignment to the RDF are:

ARMY
82nd Airborne Division, Ft. Bragg, N.C.
101st Airborne Division (Air Assault), Ft. Campbell, Ky.
24th Infantry Division (Mechanized), Ft. Stewart, Ga.
9th Infantry Division, Ft. Lewis, Wash.
6th Air Combat Cavalry Brigade, Ft. Hood, Tex.
194th Armored Brigade, Ft. Knox, Ky.
11th Air Defense Artillery Brigade, Ft. Bliss, Tex.
5th Special Forces Group and two Ranger battalions.

AIR FORCE:
27th Tactical Fighter Wing (flying F-111s), Canon AFB, N.M.
49th Tactical Fighter Wing (F-15s), Holloman AFB, N.M.
347th Tactical Fighter Wing (F-4s), Moody AFB, Ga.
354th Tactical Fighter Wing (A-10s), Myrtle Beach, S.C
23rd Tactical Fighter Wing (A-7s), England AFB, La.
552nd Airborne Warning & Control Wing (E-3A AWACS)
Strategic Projection Force, 57th Air Division (B-52H bombers; KC-135 tankers; SR-71 and U-2RS reconnaissance planes), Minot AFB, N.D.
Selected Military Airlift Command transport squadrons (C-5As, C-141s, C-130s).

MARINE CORPS:
One entire Marine Amphibious Force (MAF) composed of one Marine Division, a Marine air wing, and supporting elements.
7th Marine Amphibious Brigade (MAB), Twenty-nine Palms M.C. Base, Cal. (This unit has its heavy equipment stocked on "maritime prepositioning ships" in the Indian Ocean.)

NAVY:
Three aircraft carrier battle groups (each composed of one carrier plus three to five cruisers, destroyers, and frigates).
Three amphibious ready groups composed of helicopter assault ships (LHAs), amphibious assault ships (LPH), tank landing ships (LSTs), and other landing vessels.

(Sources: *Aviation Week & Space Technology*, February 16, 1981, pp. 86-9; and testimony of Gen. P.X. Kelley before the Subcommittee on Seapower and Force Projection of the Senate Armed Services Committee, March 9, 1981.)

"The world of the 1980s will be in many ways more demanding than the decade that we're about to conclude. Therefore President Carter and I have concluded that we must improve further our ability to deal with crises that are at a long geographical distance from us."
—Secretary of Defense Harold Brown, MacDill AFB, December 27, 1979.

up" with the supply ships, the RDF contingent would proceed to the battle zone and commence combat operations; as soon as the conflict was terminated, they would replay the whole sequence in reverse and return to their home bases in the United States, there to await the next call for their services.[11]

Although creation of the RDF would not involve the formation of any new combat units, Kelley revealed, it would require the acquisition of additional air- and sealift capabilities. As a start, the Pentagon would allocate $6 billion for procurement of 50 new long-range transport planes known as the C-X (for cargo-experimental), and would spend another $3 billion on a fleet of 15 "Maritime Prepositioning Ships" (MPS) stocked with arms and ammunition for three Marine brigades of 16,000 men each. Once outfitted, the MPS vessels would be permanently stationed in the Indian Ocean, where they would serve as a sort of "floating arsenal" for any RDF units sent to the area. When added to America's already large transport capacity, the C-X and MPS fleets would enable the Pentagon to airlift large RDF forces to the Persian Gulf and then to supply them with a full array of heavy equipment.[12]

The next step in RDF planning was announced on December 14, when Secretary Brown told a Pentagon press conference that he had established a Rapid Deployment Joint Task Force (RDJTF) at MacDill Air Force Base, Fla. to direct the new command. The RDJTF, Brown explained, "would examine the various contingencies" that might arise abroad, and "do the planning for deployment and operation of whatever parts of the rapid deployment forces were

74

to be used in a given contingency." In peacetime, this staff would be subordinated to the U.S. Readiness Command (REDCOM), but in wartime the RDJTF commander would assume operational jurisdiction over any combat forces deployed abroad.[13]

To lend substance to these plans, Brown flew to MacDill on December 27, 1979, and announced selection of General Kelley as the first RDJTF commander. He also reported that expansion of America's long-range transport capability would be a major priority in the Pentagon's budget request for Fiscal Year 1981. Recalling the "turbulence" theme described in Chapter II, Brown noted that "The world of the 1980s will be in many ways more demanding" than that of the 1970s, and thus "President Carter and I have concluded that we must improve further our ability to deal with crises that are at a long geographical distance from us."[14]

After Afghanistan

Scarcely had Brown uttered these words when Soviet forces began pouring into Afghanistan—thus transforming the strategic equation in the Persian Gulf area and forcing a re-examination of the RDF concept. Although Moscow's objective, so far as can be determined, was limited to the preservation of a client government in Kabul, the Soviet move placed Russian troops some 300 miles from the Persian Gulf coast and thus posed a hypothetical threat to Mideast oil supplies. In response, President Carter announced a build-up of U.S. forces in the Indian Ocean and, on January 23, enunciated a new strategic principle: henceforth any assault on Mideast oil supplies "will be regarded as an assault on the vital interests of the United States," and will "be repelled by any means necessary, including military force."[15]

The President's declaration, quickly dubbed the "Carter Doctrine," aroused an immediate storm of controversy. Although most U.S. leaders applauded his firm stand, some lawmakers complained that America lacked sufficient quick-reaction forces to halt a further Soviet advance toward the Gulf.[16] In response to such criticism, Administration officials assured Congress that despite some deficiencies, existing U.S. forces were fully capable of defending U.S. interests in the Gulf area. At a hastily-called press briefing, top Pentagon officials disclosed that a paratroop brigade of 4,000 men was standing by in Italy for immediate deployment to the Gulf, and that the entire 82nd Division could be moved into the area in less than two weeks. These forces would be assisted, moreover, by carrier-based aircraft and Air Force combat planes flown in from bases in Europe, Japan and the United States.[17] (See Chapter III.)

On February 21, General Kelley had his first opportunity to describe the capabilities of the RDF. "The RDJTF is here and now," he told the Senate Armed Services Committee, "and fully capable of providing our country with a wide variety of military options."[18] Kelley acknowledged that the RDF needed additional cargo planes and supply ships to be fully effective, but insisted that existing resources—which include 70 C-5A jumbo jets, 234 C-141 medium transports, and 490 C-130 tactical carriers—constitute an impressive airlift capability.[19] This capability would be enhanced, he disclosed, by the deployment of seven "Near-Term Prepositioning Ships"—merchant vessels converted to military use—in the Indian Ocean. These vessels, normally based at Diego Garcia, contain sufficient arms, ammunition, food and fuel to support a Marine Amphibious Brigade during several weeks of combat.[20]

For these units to serve as a foil to Soviet invasion forces, however, would require radical changes in the RDF concept. Originally envisioned as a light strike force for use against unsophisticated Third World armies, the RDF was obviously ill-equipped to engage Soviet-style tank forces. To meet its new responsibilities, therefore, the RDF went through a rapid transformation. Whereas the initial plan called for a lean, compact force of 100,000 soldiers, the RDF re-emerged as a much larger force equipped with a full array of heavy weapons. Any force sent to the Persian Gulf, General Kelley disclosed on June 18, 1980, would probably number 200,000 active-duty soldiers plus 100,000 reservists serving in a support capacity.[21] And because such a mammoth force could not operate without elaborate backup facilities, the once self-reliant RDF would require access to supply bases in nearby countries like Oman, Kenya, Somalia, and Egypt (each of which has signed new basing agreements with the United States).[22]

76   Even these modifications, however, did not satisfy some

*"A pre-emptive strategy to me means
that we get forces into an area rapidly,
irrespective of the size, because once you
get a force into an area that is not
occupied by the other guy, then you have
changed the whole calculus of the crisis,
and he must react to you, and you not
to him."*
—Gen. P.X. Kelley,
The Pentagon, June 18, 1980.

critics who insisted the RDF was under-equipped for any
encounter with Soviet-style armored forces. "An enhanced
ability to move U.S. ground forces quickly to the Indian
Ocean is of little avail," defense analyst Jeffrey Record
wrote in the *Washington Star*, "if the forces themselves are
improperly structured and armed to deal with potential
opponents."[23] Having expanded the RDF as much as possible within existing funding and manpower limits, General
Kelley attempted to counter this criticism by introducing an
entirely new policy for RDF employment: in place of the
original concept of a mobile "fire brigade" that would be
sent abroad in emergencies and then quickly returned to the
United States, the RDF would now serve as a sort of
"tripwire" for an open-ended U.S. commitment.

The "Pre-emptive Strategy"

As described by General Kelley on June 18, the RDF's new
"pre-emptive strategy" calls for an immediate troop deployment at the first indication of a *possible* Soviet incursion, in order to signal U.S. determination and thus, hope-
fully, discourage any further Russian moves. The attraction
of this new approach, Kelley affirmed, is that the initial RDF
detachment needn't be particularly large or powerful—
it need only suggest the likelihood of further U.S. moves.
"Once you get a force into an area that is not occupied by
the other guy," he explained, "then you have changed the
whole calculus of the crisis, and he must react to you, not
you to him." Even if the first-arriving U.S. forces were not

77

equipped to fight Soviet armored units, the implied threat of U.S. escalation should be adequate to persuade Moscow to "bow out gracefully." And should the initial deployment prove insufficiently threatening, the RDJTF could expand this force indefinitely. "There's no upper limit," Kelley avowed, "to the Rapid Deployment Joint Task Force capability."[24]

Adoption of a "pre-emptive strategy" obviously raises serious questions about RDF planning. Just how far is Washington prepared to go in fighting a Mideast war? Kelley himself said that there's no "upper limit" on RDF troop strength, and his boss, Gen. Volney F. Warner of REDCOM, said on October 28, 1980, that the 82nd Airborne Division and a Marine brigade would not be "too big a force to lose" in a Mideast conflict.[25] And then there's the question of tactical nuclear weapons. General Kelley once remarked that "I wouldn't touch that [issue] with a ten-foot pole," but other Pentagon leaders have not been so reticent: one high official admitted in February 1980 that "we are thinking of theater nuclear options" in the event that RDF forces are outnumbered on the battlefield, and former Secretary of Defense James R. Schlesinger told students at Georgetown University in May 1981 that the Pentagon must consider "the employment, or the threat of employment, of tactical nuclear weapons" in the event of a Persian Gulf war.[26] It is not too hard to deduce from all of this that even a token RDF deployment to the Gulf area could produce a superpower confrontation and thence spark a global nuclear war.

Given this frightening prospect, U.S. policymakers would appear well advised to ponder the risks of a pre-emptive policy. Nevertheless, subsequent debate on the RDF has focused almost exclusively on the perennial issue of adequacy. "Even if these divisions could be transported in time to the Indian Ocean," Schlesinger observed in late 1980, it is scarcely evident with what they would fight and what forces they could overcome.[27] Although Pentagon officials continued to insist on the adequacy of existing plans—"The Rapid Deployment Force is not a paper tiger," General Kelley affirmed on October 1, 1980[28]—they have failed to persuade the growing army of skeptics. Finally, when the Iran-Iraq war accentuated the continuing vulnerability of Mideast oil supplies, Secretary Brown acquiesced to yet another expansion of RDF strength. In September 1980, George Wilson of the *Washington Post* reported that "Pentagon leaders, apparently stung by criticism that the Rapid Deployment Force promises too little too late for the Persian Gulf, have launched an effort to beef it up in a hurry."[29] One product of this effort was the creation of a "Strategic Projection Force"—a squadron of B-52H intercontinental bombers armed with conventional bombs which can be flown from bases in the United States directly to the Persian Gulf (with refueling stops in Spain and other European bases). According to Air Force officials, this force could be "on station" in the Gulf area within 36 hours of a go-ahead signal from the RDF commander.[30]

Even this addition, and other improvements ordered by Secretary Brown, were not enough to satisfy the incoming Administration of Ronald Reagan. Throughout the campaign, Reagan vowed tht he would take whatever steps are necessary to protect vital overseas interests, and his Secretary of Defense, Caspar Weinberger, has placed top emphasis on improving U.S. "readiness" for combat abroad. The Administration's revised Fiscal 1981-82 Defense Budget, released on March 4, 1981, earmarked $11.6 billion specifically for "readiness," which Weinberger defined as "items which increase the near-term capability of our forces to react to contingency situations, to deploy or redeploy rapidly and efficiently, and to sustain combat operations."[31] Needless to say, the principal beneficiary of these funds is the Rapid Deployment Force.

Although Reagan has retained the basic RDF concept as it evolved in the Carter Administration—i.e., a "reservoir" of U.S.-based forces available for rapid deployment to Third World conflict zones—it has radically altered the RDF's command structure and jurisdictional authority. On April 24, 1981, Defense Secretary Weinberger announced that instead of forming a subordinate organization under the aegis of the Readiness Command (REDCOM), as envisioned by former Secretary Brown, the RDF would evolve into a full-scale "unified command" with jurisdiction over the Persian Gulf area. As in the case of existing unified commands—the European Command, the Pacific Command, and the Southern (Latin American) Command—the new RDF headquarters (to be called the Middle East Command or Southwest Asia Command) will exercise "operational control" over all U.S. forces in its area of responsibility. (Ultimately, the new command will establish a headquarters complex in the Gulf area—either on land, at one of the bases in Oman, Somalia, or Egypt recently acquired by the United States, or at sea, on one of the World War II-vintage battleships now being reactivated by the Reagan Administration—but for now the RDJTF will remain at MacDill AFB in Florida.[32]) To oversee the transition to a unified command, Weinberger named Army Gen. Robert Kingston—a former Green Beret officer with extensive Vietnam War experience—to succeed Gen. Kelley as RDF commander.

The elevation of the RDF from a subordinate strike force into a full-scale joint command is yet another product of the momentum in RDF growth that has characterized the force since its inception in 1977. This momentum has carried it from conception to reality in record time, and promises even greater expansion in the years ahead. And if this momentum persists, one final transformation appears almost inevitable: the leap from force-in-readiness to force-in-being. Like the Green Berets of Kennedy's day, the RDF is *an army in search of a war.*

And the chances of finding a war must be considered exceptionally high. Not only is the Third World simmering with a host of conflicts which could easily ignite in full-scale violence, but the Reagan entourage also appears committed to the use of force as a standard instrument of U.S. policy. "A Reagan Administration is going to act a good deal more aggressively" in combatting Third World guerrillas, Roger Fontaine of the National Security Council staff told the *Miami Herald* in 1980.[33] Reagan's advisers have also declared that Washington will use force if necessary to defend Persian Gulf oil supplies, as affirmed by the "Carter Doctrine," and will likewise consider military action to protect imports of other critical materials, as envisioned by the "Haig Doctrine." (See Chapters III and IV.) Administration rhetoric suggests, moreover, that Reagan is prepared to order military action against Cuba, in the event of a Cuban-sponsored insurrection in Latin America, or against Libya, in the event of a new Libyan intervention in Africa. If these views prevail—and there is every reason to assume they will—then it will only be a matter of time before some flareup somewhere in the Third World triggers the first

80

"Because of technical advances in weaponry and the great mobility of armies today, a future largescale war overseas will probably begin and end very rapidly and produce casualties at a higher rate than any other war in history."

—U.S. Dept. of Defense
brochure on the Civilian-Military Contingency
Hospital System
(CMCHS), 1981.

appearance in battle of the Rapid Deployment Force.

But while the actual use of the RDF in some Third World conflict may provide a psychological boost to those Reagan followers who decried the "vacillation and appeasement" of the Carter Administration, it is not likely to solve any of our major foreign policy difficulties. Most military analysts agree, for instance, that any U.S. effort to "seize Arab oil" would probably result in the total destruction of Mideast oil facilities and bring on a global depression (see Chapter III). A U.S. intervention in El Salvador, meanwhile, could easily provoke a region-wide guerrilla war that would prove as debilitating and futile as the conflict in Vietnam. And given the high cost of fuel and other military "consumables," a prolonged U.S. engagement in the Third World is likely to cost far more than any economic interests it is supposedly designed to protect (the Vietnam war, for instance, would cost $1 trillion at today's prices) and produce a new round of inflation that would cripple the U.S. economy.

There are also important political risks attached to such a posture. Since Vietnam, Third World countries have become more and more united in their opposition to military intervention by the superpowers. Any U.S. incursion in these areas is thus likely to trigger the same sort of universal condemnation that greeted the Soviet invasion of Afghanistan. And then there is the homefront to consider: although most adult Americans now appear to favor a more assertive military policy abroad, it is likely that anything even remotely resembling a replay of Vietnam will produce instan-

81

taneous and widespread opposition—especially if, as is likely, Reagan had to reinstate the draft in order to produce the extra soldiers that would be needed for such an operation.

Most worrisome, however, are the military risks of such action. Largely as a result of the booming arms trade (in which the United States is a major supplier), Third World armies are now far better equipped than they were ten or even five years ago. Many of our most likely adversaries—countries like Libya, Syria, Iraq, and South Yemen—are armed with the most advanced French, British, Russian (and even, in some cases, American) arms available on the world market. Any U.S. forces sent to war in these areas are therefore likely to encounter far tougher resistance than they ever faced in Southeast Asia.* It is precisely for this reason that Pentagon officials have raised the possibility of using tactical nuclear weapons to defend outnumbered RDF forces sent abroad. And it is not hard to imagine how even a "limited" use of tactical nukes could escalate into a full-scale nuclear war.

The evolution of RDF forces from initial concept to the present, full-bodied reality represents an extraordinary odyssey. For many Americans, this achievement constitutes a welcome antidote to the frustrations engendered by the hostage crisis and other foreign policy reversals. But it is one thing to talk about the advantages of rapid deployment, and another to commit troops to actual warfare. Once U.S. forces arrive on an overseas battlefield, we set off a chain of events whose final outcome can never be foreseen. Because such action could easily trigger a wider war, it is essential that the American public reconsider its commitment to the RDF before we find ourselves in an uncontrolled conflagration.

---

*Indeed, so heavy are the casualties expected to be in such a confrontation that the military medical system will rapidly become overloaded, and so the Pentagon has asked civilian hospitals throughout the United States to develop contingency plans for the care of wounded soldiers flown back to the United States. In announcing this program, known as the Civilian-Military Contingency Hospital System (CMCHS), the Department of Defense noted that "Because of technical advances in weaponry and the great mobility of armies today, a future large-scale war overseas will probably begin and end very rapidly and *produce casualties at a higher rate than any other war in history*."[34] (Emphasis added.)

VI:
WASHINGTON PREPARES FOR "A SECOND VIETNAM": THE RESURRECTION OF COUNTERINSURGENCY

Just six years after the end of the Vietnam War, American military advisers were again committed to a guerrilla conflict in the Third World. Citing a Soviet-backed effort to topple the pro-U.S. junta in El Salvador, Secretary of State Alexander Haig announced on March 2, 1981, that Washington was sending another two dozen advisers to join the 30 or so already aiding government forces in their conflict with Salvadorean guerrillas. And while Haig insisted that the United States was not embarking on "a second Vietnam" as charged by some Congressional critics, one of his aides confirmed that the U.S. advisory group in El Salvador includes "a counterinsurgency operational planning and assistance team."[1]

Counterinsurgency. Perhaps no word more vividly describes the military priorities of the 1960s, when President Kennedy's obsession with guerrilla warfare led us inexorably into the Indochina war. After Vietnam, no word disappeared more quickly from the military lexicon, as Washington adopted a new foreign policy based on negotiation and non-interventionism. Instead of focusing on problems of "brushfire wars" and "unconventional operations," the Pentagon turned its attention to the revitalization of NATO and other "post-Vietnam" priorities. But now, as the Reagan Administration places renewed emphasis on meeting the threat of revolutionary conflict in the

Third World, counterinsurgency is again sweeping into fashion in Washington.

As defined by Kennedy's advisers, counterinsurgency encompassed all those political, economic, and military efforts undertaken by the United States to defeat revolutionary guerrillas in their preferred (usually tropical) environment. To conduct such operations, the Pentagon established a host of "special" organizations, including the Army's Special Forces (the "Green Berets"), the Navy's SEAL (sea/air/land) commandos, and the Air Force's Special Operations Force (SOF). In the heyday of counterinsurgency, these units were deployed in scores of countries, including Bolivia, Colombia, Guatemala, Thailand, Indonesia, Laos and the Philippines.[2] After Vietnam, however, many of these units were disbanded or reduced in strength, and those that survived turned away from counterinsurgency in search of more fashionable pursuits. Ever since the beginning of the Iranian hostage crisis, however, there has been a spectacular rebirth of interest in special operations. As Rep. Charles E. Bennett of the House Armed Services Committee observed in late 1980, "Many recent events worldwide should lead us to believe that unconventional warfare forces may well become an increasingly important element in our defense equation."[3]

The resurgence of interest in counterinsurgency first began during the closing months of the Carter Administration—as reflected in growing U.S. arms aid to government forces in El Salvador—but has acquired added momentum since President Reagan moved into the White House. Jeane Kirkpatrick, Reagan's choice for U.S. Ambassador to the United Nations, has already warned that the new Administration will be far more vigorous than the old in combatting "Castroite" guerrillas in Central America.[4] Secretary of State Alexander Haig told reporters on January 28 that "international terrorism"—the Administration's euphemism for revolutionary and insurgent conflict—"will take the place of human rights in our concern." And another Reagan adviser, Roger Fontaine of the National Security Council, told the *Miami Herald* that if stepped-up military aid fails to eliminate the guerrilla threat to pro-U.S. regimes in Latin America, "the use of military force is an option" that Reagan "has to maintain as a possibility."[5]

84   Although the new infatuation with counterinsurgency

has not yet reached the proportions of the Kennedy era, signs of its vitality are manifold:

• The Joint Chiefs of Staff have established a new Joint Special Operations Command (JSOC) at Fort Bragg to coordinate activities of the services' various "special" units. Creation of the new command, headed by Brig. Gen. Richard A. Scholtes of the Army's 18th Airborne Corps, suggests a growing interest in counterinsurgency at the highest Pentagon levels.[6]

• Despite protests by church leaders and Congressional critics, Washington has continued to pour arms and ammunition into El Salvador, and to expand the U.S. advisory presence. Among the personnel deployed in El Salvador is a team of 15 Army Green Berets, whose mission reportedly includes training Salvadorean troops in "communications, logistics, and intelligence."[7] Reagan also plans to increase U.S. military aid to Honduras, Guatemala, and other Central American countries facing possible insurgent uprisings.

• Elsewhere in the Third World, U.S. aid is again flowing to pro-U.S. regimes facing indigenous guerrilla movements. The new Fiscal 1982 military aid request features substantial increases for Thailand, Indonesia, and the Philippines—all of which have long been engaged in U.S.-supported counterinsurgency campaigns against domestic dissidents—along with fresh outlays for such countries as Oman, Tunisia, and Morocco.[8]

• After years of stressing NATO scenarios, the Pentagon has quietly stepped up training for guerrilla-type engagements. The Marines have established a new jungle warfare training base in Guam, and the Army has conducted its own jungle exercises in the Panama Canal Zone. And, according to ABC News, the Pentagon has also conducted a series of simulated commando operations in the American Southwest, presumably involving Green Berets, Black Berets (the Army's "Ranger" battalions), and the super-secret "Blue Light" anti-terrorist force based at Fort Bragg.[9]

• With the formation of the Rapid Deployment Force (RDF), the United States now has—for the first time since Vietnam—a large force configured specifically for intervention in non-NATO contingencies. And while the new unit's principal function will be protection of the oil flow from the Middle East, RDF components are also being trained for counterguerrilla operations in other areas, including

Central America and the Caribbean. It is also noteworthy that President Reagan selected a former Green Beret officer—Gen. Robert Kingston—to assume command of the RDF in 1981.

● In recognition of the growing threat of *urban* insurgencies such as those experienced in Northern Ireland and Teheran, the Army recently joined with the American Defense Preparedness Association in sponsoring a symposium on "Military Operations in Built-Up Areas." The meeting, classified CONFIDENTIAL, was held at the Harry Diamond Laboratories in Adelphi, Md., and featured talks by American, British, and West German officers.[10]

These steps, and others of a similar nature, indicate a growing commitment to unconventional warfare at the highest policy-making levels in Washington. Such moves are being accompanied, moreover, by a *political* effort to rehabilitate counterinsurgency as a legitimate instrument of military policy. In a recent issue of the *Naval Institute Proceedings*, for instance, two former counterinsurgency specialists wrote that "During the next 20 years, revolutions, civil wars, ethnic hostilities, border wars, and proxy conflicts will be the order of the day," and that only special forces offer "a means of resolving [such] disputes while tiptoeing around the nuclear trip-wire." This article was subsequently inserted in the *Congressional Record* by Rep. Bennett, who affirmed in a preamble that special forces "provide us with a unique capability to meet challenges of an unconventional and destructive nature."[11]

These views, shared by many strategists in Reagan's entourage, are certain to become official doctrine in the not-too-distant future. And if the experience of the 1960s is any indication—when Kennedy's preoccupation with guerrilla warfare led us into Vietnam—the new infatuation with counterinsurgency is likely to produce equally dire results. Judging by present trends, the U.S. could soon be sucked into new military adventures in such locales as Central America, northern Africa, the Arabian Peninsula, and, once again, Southeast Asia. But before discussing these potential flashpoints, it is important to show how counterinsurgency doctrine itself is being refurbished in order to eliminate the many fallacies exposed in Vietnam and to prepare for the likely contingencies of the 1980s.

The Evolution of Counterinsurgency Doctrine

As originally conceived by strategists of the Kennedy era, counterinsurgency involved a two-pronged campaign to defeat the guerrillas and to buttress shaky regimes in the Third World.[12]

● First, a *military effort* designed to locate insurgent cells and forces, to isolate them from the rest of the population, and thence to destroy them with superior firepower and technology. Primary responsibility for this effort was to be assumed by the host country's own military and police forces, supported, where necessary, by U.S. advisers and technicians.

● Second, a *political-economic effort* (sometimes known as the "other war") designed to redress local grievances and to improve the material well-being of the subject population—and thereby generate popular support for the prevailing government. This effort, often described as "winning hearts and minds," was considered the responsiblity of civilian agencies working with technical advisers recruited from American universities and other non-government organizations.

Essential to this approach was the assumption that the government involved, while possibly corrupt or undemocratic in some respects, could be encouraged to make the reforms necessary to elicit public support. "Far from being a blank check to worthless oligarchies," counterinsurgency strategist Charles Maechling once observed, "counterinsurgency doctrine is predicated on political and economic reform."[13] And, because the United States viewed itself as an ally rather than a colonial power, this model further assumed that the host government would assume primary responsiblity for the counterinsurgency effort while American involvement would be limited as much as possible to advisory and supply functions.

As the Vietnam War unfolded, these assumptions proved hopelessly fallacious as U.S. forces were drawn into a prolonged and futile crusade to save the corrupt Saigon regime. Although Washington attempted to dominate the battlefield through continuously escalating dosages of firepower, the original principles of counterinsurgency were abandoned long before U.S. troops were finally withdrawn from Indochina.[14]

For some U.S. strategists, the experience of Vietnam was so traumatic that they ceased believing in counterinsurgency altogether and turned instead to more conventional strategic problems such as the defense of Western Europe. "The most notable developments in military thought about Third World contingencies," Professor Robert E. Osgood of Johns Hopkins University observed in 1979, has been "the shift from the confidence of the 1960s . . . to the present prevailing doubts about the ability of the United States to intervene effectively" in guerrilla-type conflicts.[15] Nonetheless, some strategists refused to concede defeat and, as recounted by Osgood in *Limited War Revisited*, attempted to absorb the "lessons of Vietnam" and to fashion a new counterinsurgency doctrine based on a more realistic view of insurgent conflict.

Although no fully-developed body of doctrine has as yet evolved to replace the strategies of the Kennedy period, examination of recent military exercises and policy debates indicates that some common themes have begun to emerge. Fundamental to these new policies is a vastly altered outlook regarding the fundamental assumptions of counterinsurgency. Missing from this approach is any view of the counterinsurgent as a glorified Peace Corps worker whose principal function is to woo sympathetic peasants away from the alien philosophies of Ho Chi Minh and "Che" Guevara. Whereas strategists of the Kennedy era believed that the success of their efforts depended largely on this *political* struggle for the "hearts and minds" of Third World peoples, today's counterinsurgents tend to rely almost exclusively on military means to overcome the insurgents. Gone, too, are any illusions about promoting reform on the part of Third World governments—today's counterinsurgency partners are chosen for their perseverence under fire, not their commitment to social and economic progress. And in place of the educational and development programs of the "other war," today's counterinsurgents emphasize the use of modern technology to enhance the government's military advantage over the insurgents.

Arising out of this cynical and mechanistic outlook are the following components of the new counterinsurgency:

"Effective policing is like 'preventive medicine.' The police can deal with threats to internal order in their formative stages. Should they not be prepared to do this, 'major surgery' would be needed to redress these threats. This action is painful and expensive and disruptive in itself."
—Under Secretary of State U. Alexis Johnson, *Dept. of State Bulletin*, September 13, 1971.

1. *"Preventive Medicine"*: Rather than wait until the insurgents are armed and active to initiate military countermeasures, current counterinsurgency doctrine calls for the identification, arrest, and imprisonment (or outright assassination) of suspected dissidents *before* they can organize insurgent cells. To be successful, these efforts require the constant scrutiny of citizen behavior by the police and government informers, along with the use of modern eavesdropping, surveillance, and data-processing systems. Such measures, which have become commonplace in many of the Third World countries ruled by martial law, are described as "preventive medicine" by U.S. strategists because in theory they preclude the need for full-scale military intervention of the sort witnessed in Vietnam. "Effective policing is like 'preventive medicine,'" former Under Secretary of State U. Alexis Johnson once observed. "The police can deal with threats to internal order in their formative stages. Should they not be prepared to do this, 'major surgery' would be needed to redress these threats. This action is painful and expensive and disruptive in itself."[16]

2. *Urban Counterinsurgency:* Whereas earlier counterinsurgency strategies were concerned almost exclusively with the threat of rural guerrilla warfare, current doctrine places much more emphasis on the problem of urban insurrection. This shift reflects both the growing urbanization of Third World societies, plus the fact that revolutionary movements are increasingly aiming their organizing efforts at the underemployed and impoverished inhabitants

of the shantytowns which encircle most Third World cities. In many of these countries, warns Professor Lucian Pye of M.I.T., "the teeming urban populations are so highly politicizied that they have become in a sense loaded revolvers pointed at the responsible governments."[17] To preserve order in the face of these "revolvers," U.S. strategists favor the creation of omnipresent, militarized police forces equipped with a sophisticated arsenal of riot-control and anti-terrorist munitions. This approach, already fully tested in cities like Buenos Aires, Belfast and Manila, is now being refined for use in other countries—including many in the industrialized world—that are likely to experience urban disorders in the years ahead.[18]

3. *Rapid Deployment*: Whereas Kennedy's advisers urged a restrained and *gradual* military buildup in Indochina—to preserve the myth of South Vietnamese leadership in the counterguerrilla struggle—today's counterinsurgents universally believe in the need for a massive and *rapid* deployment of troops in order to overcome insurgent forces before they can win support from the indigenous population and thus trigger the kind of protracted (and ultimately futile) struggle encountered in Vietnam. This principle is explicitly recognized in the designation of America's new interventionary army as a *Rapid Deployment Force*, and in recent exercises involving the airlift of U.S.-based troops to potential conflict zones in the Middle East. To deal with future Third World crises, outgoing Secretary of Defense Harold Brown affirmed in 1980, our needs "center not so much on additional combat forces as on our ability to move suitably trained and equipped forces over great distances quickly enough so that they can be of real use at the point of crisis."[19]

4. *Massive Firepower*: In line with the objective of destroying insurgent forces quickly, counterinsurgency strategists now believe that government troops should immediately employ the full range of weapons at their disposal rather than to escalate slowly up the military ladder. While many analysts had once argued that an excessive reliance on firepower contributed to the U.S. defeat in Vietnam, today's counterinsurgents argue that a heavy dosage of firepower *early* in the war would have eliminated guerrilla forces while they were still weak, whereas the gradual escalation actually employed by U.S. forces allowed the

Viet Cong to survive and grow—thus forcing Washington to escalate much higher than would otherwise have been necessary. "The result of gradualism in Vietnam" Osgood observed in 1979, "was to permit the war to drag on at increasing cost and public opposition without the satisfaction of anticipating a clear-cut victory;" it is possible to conclude, therefore, "that the United States could and should have won the war by earlier and more extensive escalation."[20] This "lesson," as Osgood puts it, is sure to be honored by the Rapid Deployment Force, which is likely to employ the full range of U.S. weapons at the very onset of any future intervention in the Third World. And if conventional weapons fail to produce an early and economical victory, Pentagon officials concede that they are "thinking of theater nuclear weapons" to ensure success in such encounters.[21]

These principles, while not as fully articulated as those of the Kennedy era, are part of what is rapidly becoming a unified counterinsurgency doctrine. It is increasingly apparent, moreover, that this doctrine will see widespread application in the years ahead. The creation of the Rapid Deployment Force, the recent RDF exercises in Egypt, and the other developments described earlier, all suggest that Washington is increasingly prepared to engage in military intervention when and where such action is deemed necessary.

The Potential Battlefields

The only remaining questions are *when* and *where* U.S. forces will be sent into combat. While no one can respond with any degree of certainty, several Third World conflicts appear particularly inviting to U.S. counterinsurgents:

● *El Salvador*, where U.S.-backed government forces are fighting a loose coalition of opposition groups known as the Democratic Revolutionary Front. U.S. counterinsurgency specialists are already operating in El Salvador, and Reagan has pledged to deploy still more military advisers along with stepped-up arms deliveries. Because the Salvadorean conflict could easily spill over into neighboring Honduras and Nicaragua, it is altogether possible that U.S. involvement could eventually escalate into a regional conflagration.[22]

● *Oman*, where the country's autocratic ruler, Sultan

Qaboos bin Said, has long been engaged in a counterinsurgency conflict with rebel forces in Dhofar Province. Although the insurgents, organized as the Popular Front for the Liberation of Oman and the Arabian Gulf (PFLOAG), were largely defeated in the mid-1970s by combined Omani, Jordanian, and Iranian forces operating out of Salalah, Dhofar Province was never fully pacified and there have been reports of stepped-up guerrilla activity (usually ascribed, in official communiques, to meddling by the Soviet-equipped forces of neighboring Southern Yemen). Because Iran is no longer prepared to serve as "regional gendarme," Sultan Qaboos has turned to the United States for additional military aid; and because Washington seeks bases in the Persian Gulf area to serve as staging areas for the RDF, such aid has been steadily growing. U.S. advisers are already assisting the Sultan's Armed Forces, and it is possible that larger U.S. contingents will be sent in the near future. And if the PFLOAG guerrillas are ever joined by Yemeni forces—a not impossible scenario, given the historical enmity between Oman and Yemen—U.S. intervention is almost foreordained. As Capt. Richard A. Stewart of the Marine Corps noted in a recent issue of *Naval Institute Proceedings*, "Epic events in this critical but unstable region could make Oman, Muscat, and Salalah as familiar as Inchon, Da Nang, or Teheran."[23]

● *The Western Sahara*, where Moroccan forces have been fighting a grueling desert war against guerrillas of the Polisario Front. Originally a Spanish territory, this phosphate-rich area was occupied by Morocco and Mauritania when abandoned by Madrid in 1976. The indigenous, largely nomadic population was never consulted in the turnover, and has resisted Moroccan occupation ever since (the Mauritanians bowed out of the conflict in 1978). At first, Washington refused to recognize Moroccan sovereignty over the Western Sahara, and turned down King Hassan's requests for counterinsurgency equipment; in 1980, however, President Carter (under heavy prodding from Zbigniew Brzezinski) overruled the State Department and approved the sale of six Rockwell OV-10 "Bronco" counterinsurgency planes and 24 Hughes 500-MD helicopter gunships for use in the Saharan war. Although the U.S. presence is now limited to a few technicians and advisers, it could easily expand as the Reagan Administration steps up support for the eminently pro-Western King Hassan.[24]

● *Angola and Zaire*, where the United States has intermittently been involved in local guerrilla conflicts. In Angola, U.S. aid will probably resume to anti-government forces in the north and south; such aid was banned by the Clark Amendment to the 1976 foreign aid bill, but may soon resume if new legislation introduced by the Reagan Administration is adopted by Congress. The White House has already promised to remove existing restraints on covert actions by the CIA, and it is likely that Angola—ruled by a Marxist regime with Cuban military assistance—will prove an early target for such operations. Across the border in Zaire, insurgent forces have twice staged insurrections in mineral-rich Shaba Province, and in both cases U.S. combat-support units were used to supply the French, Belgian, and Moroccan forces brought in to restore order. Despite intensive efforts to improve Zairian military capabilities, the region is still unstable, and U.S. forces may well be employed in the event of another Shaba uprising.[25]

● *Libya, Chad, and Sudan*, where pro-Western and pro-Soviet forces have been engaged in continuing skirmishing over the past few years (along with French and Egyptian forces, which have sometimes been sent to aid one side or another in these conflicts). The Reagan Administration has not disguised its hostility for Libyan leader Col. Muammar Qaddafi (who recently sent troops into Chad), and has pledged to aid any African country threatened by Libyan "intervention." In a 1981 policy address, Assistant Secretary of State Chester Crocker avowed that the Administration was "determined to be supportive of those states that wish to resist what Libya has done in Chad."[26]

● *Southeast Asia*, where long-simmering guerrilla conflicts in Burma, Thailand, Indonesia, and the Philippines may invite U.S. participation. Although most U.S. leaders once adopted a "never again" stance on the use of American combat forces in this volatile area, U.S. military aid has risen steadily over the past few years and it is only a matter of time before U.S. advisers are introduced in significant numbers. And while Washington is undoubtedly wary of any major commitment, the growing concern over guerrilla warfare could eventually impel U.S. leaders to risk another protracted guerrilla conflict.

At this point, it is still too early to determine which of

these areas will serve as the next major proving ground for counterinsurgency. What *is* certain is that most of the inhibitions which once barred Washington from embarking upon another Vietnam are no longer in operation. As noted by defense analyst William M. Arkin, "nothing so symbolizes the demise of the 'Vietnam Syndrome' as the current effort to resuscitate counterinsurgency."[27]

And nothing should so frighten Americans as the current revival of counterinsurgency. Once before, in the early 1960s, a President's obsession with guerrilla combat led us into a calamitous war; now, with another President eager to revive the counterinsurgency establishment, we face the certain risk of another disaster. Indeed, for anyone familiar with recent history, the current U.S. buildup in El Salvador and the Mideast appears only too similar to the initial U.S. buildup in Southeast Asia. First come the advisers to provide training in counterinsurgency; then come more "advisers" to accompany allied troops on combat missions; then regular troops to protect the "advisers"; then more troops to support the first batch; and then it's just a short step to full-scale war. So far, Washington has only taken the first few steps in this direction; if the revival of counterinsurgency is not halted, however, it will only be a matter of time before the remaining steps take us all the way to catastrophe.

EPILOGUE:

EL SALVADOR AND BEYOND: THE PERSISTENCE OF THE "SYNDROME" (AND WHAT YOU CAN DO TO HELP)

On March 2, 1981, the recently-installed Administration of Ronald Reagan announced that it was stepping up U.S. military assistance to the despotic rulers of El Salvador in order to demonstrate that Washington would no longer "sit by passively" in the face of armed insurgency in Latin America. Included in the Administration's emergency aid package was $25 million worth of arms and ammunition, along with twenty more U.S. military advisers. The advisers, members of the Army's Special Forces, were sent to provide counterinsurgency training to the Salvadorean Army—which has been credited, by church sources, with the murder of at least 9,000 unarmed civilians in the past year alone. For many observers, the Reagan move constituted the opening salvo in what has been called America's "second Vietnam."

In response to widespread criticism of its Central America policy, the Reagan Administration has affirmed that it does not contemplate "another Vietnam" in El Salvador involving the deployment of regular U.S. combat troops. "I certainly don't see us going in with fighting forces," Reagan told CBS newsman Walter Cronkite on March 3rd. Despite such assurances, the El Salvador situation has been interpreted by many as a test of the Administration's determination to surmount the Vietnam Syndrome and to revive military intervention as a legitimate instrument of U.S. foreign policy—an interpretation culti-vated by the Administration itself. "The problem here is a

95

critical one for the American people," Secretary of State Alexander Haig told the editors of *Time* magazine on March 16. "That is, whether or not we are going to turn our back" on such revolutionary challenges.

But if Reagan, Haig & Co. believed that the American people would instantly embrace an interventionist course, they were in for a rude awakening. Not only have most Americans opposed U.S. intervention in El Salvador (Congressional sources report that mail from constituents has been running twenty-to-one against the Administration's aid program), but many influential religious organizations, including the National Conference of Roman Catholic Bishops, have campaigned actively against further military assistance. Thus, on March 5, 1981, Washington Archbishop James A. Hickey testified before the House Foreign Affairs Subcommittee on Inter-American Affairs in vigorous opposition to further military aid to El Salvador, which he said would confirm suspicions "that we are slowly preparing for an invasion of El Salvador."

Spirited opposition to U.S. intervention has also surfaced in the Congress, despite a determined Administration effort to mobilize "bipartisan" support for its hard-lined policy. On March 3, the day after Reagan's $25 million aid package was announced, some 45 Congresspersons sent a telegram to the President opposing further military assistance to the Salvadorean junta in unusually strong terms: "There is no evidence that the Salvadorean government has brought is security forces under responsible control, and training these forces will simply provide them with the expertise to continue their brutal violation of human rights."

Nor has this been the full extent of public opposition to Reagan's El Salvador policy. Many newspapers have issued editorials condemning the military aid program, many campuses have hosted well-attended teach-ins on the subject, and, on May 3, 1981, some 100,000 people of all ages, colors, and backgrounds marched to the Pentagon in the largest demonstration of antiwar sentiment since the end of the Vietnam War (another 25,000 people marched in a similar protest in San Francisco). Indeed, by mid-1981, the Reagan Administration confronted a nationwide movement against intervention in El Salvador that has surprised many by its intensity and broad-based participation. It appears, therefore, that all those declarations about the complete disappearance of the Vietnam Syndrome have been somewhat premature.

The El Salvador case cannot, of course, be considered an accurate barometer of U.S. reactions to *any* potential intervention abroad. It is likely, for instance, that the public would applaud military action in the event of another hostage takeover like the one that occurred in Iran, or in some other clearcut instance of violence against American citizens. But the degree of support for other hypothetical moves—an "energy war" in Saudi Arabia, for instance, or a "resource war" in Southern Africa—remains problematical at this point. For, despite all the traumas of the past few years and a continuing government effort to mobilize suppot for a more aggressive military posture, the public retains its repugnance for Vietnam-type interventions in the Third World. And so long as this repugnance persists, U.S. leaders will be very reluctant to commit U.S. forces to combat abroad.

If, as argued in the preceding chapters, an interventionist posture risks global conflagration and the loss of all those "vital interests" such a posture would supposedly protect, then the Vietnam Syndrome is an essential feature of U.S. national security and economic survival. Our moral and political values are also at stake: by preventing unwarranted intervention in other countries' internal disputes, the Syndrome protects us from the imperial excesses and anti-democratic tendencies which were exposed by the Watergate scandal. It follows, then, that most Americans have a vested interest in the survival of a non-interventionist policy. But the Syndrome will not persist forever without conspicuous public reaffirmation. Citizen action is needed, therefore, to remind U.S. leaders of its continued validity. Such action is the *surest way* to guarantee that we will not be dragged into a catastrophic replay of Vietnam.

How do we go about this? There is much that one can do as an individual: send a letter or telegram to Members of Congress expressing opposition to U.S. aid to El Salvador or other forms of military intervention abroad; write a letter to the editor of a local newspaper or magazine; submit a guest editorial (or "op-ed piece") to the same periodicals; organize a symposium or debate in neighborhood school, church or civic institution. Experience suggests, however, that one can accomplish a great deal more by working together with other people in grass-roots organizations and coalitions. Such groups can conduct more ambitious and visible activities, including: teach-ins and rallies; lobbying efforts in Washington and state capitals; petition campaigns; vigils, marches, and other forms of public protest. To find out how you can participate in local and national efforts on behalf of a non-interventionist foreign policy, contact:

- *The Coalition for a New Foreign & Military Policy*, 120 Maryland Ave. N.E., Washington, D.C. 20002.
- *American Friends Service Committee*, 1501 Cherry St., Philadelphia, PA 19102.
- *Mobilization for Survival*, 3601 Locust Walk, Philadelphia, PA 19104.
- *Alliance for Survival*, 1473 Echo Park Ave., Los Angles, CA 90026.
- *Women Strike for Peace*, 145 South 13th St., Philadelphia, PA 19107.
- *Women's International League for Peace and Freedom*, 1213 Race St., Philadelphia, PA 19107.
- *Clergy and Laity Concerned*, 198 Broadway, New York, NY 10038.
- *Fellowship of Reconciliation*, P.O. Box 271, Nyack, NY 10961.
- *SANE*, 514 C St., N.E., Washington, D.C. 20002.
- *Committee Against Registration and the Draft*, 245 2nd St., N.E., Washington, D.C. 20002.
- *War Resisters League*, 339 Lafayette St., New York, NY 10012.
- *Riverside Church Disarmament Program*, 490 Riverside Dr., New York, NY 10027.
- *Sojourners Peace Ministry*, 1309 L St., N.W., Washinghton, D.C. 20005.
- *World Peacemakers*, 2852 Ontario Rd., N.W., Washington, D.C. 20009.

Organizations which provide educational materials on peace and disarmament (in addition to those listed above) include:

- *Institute for Policy Studies*, 1901 Que St., N.W., Washington, D.C. 20009.

- *Center for Defense Information*, 120 Maryland Ave., N.E., Washington, D.C. 20002.
- *Center for International Policy*, 120 Maryland Ave., N.E., Washington, D.C. 20002.
- NARMIC, c/o American Friends Service Committee, 1501 Cherry St., Philadelphia, PA 19102.
- *Friends Committee on National Legislation*, 245 2nd St., N.E., Washington, D.C. 20002.
- *Institute for World Order*, 777 United Nations Plaza, New York, NY 10017.

FOOTNOTES

Chapter I

1. The concept of a concerted campaign to erase the Vietnam Syndrome was first explored by the author in: "Curing the Vietnam Syndrome," *The Nation* (Oct. 13, 1979), pp. 321, 337-40.

2. Quoted in *The Defense Monitor*, Vol. IV, No. 7 (September, 1975), p. 5.

3. James Schlesinger, "A Testing Time for America," *Fortune* (February, 1976), p. 76.

4. "The Decline of U.S. Power," *Business Week* (March 12, 1979), p. 88.

5. Extracts from Schlesinger, "A Testing Time for America," pp. 74-77; and "The Decline of U.S. Power," pp. 36-96.

6. George Will, "No More 'No More Vietnams,'" *Newsweek* (March 19, 1979), p. 104.

7. The Baker quote is from "The Decline of U.S. Power," p. 88; the Jackson quote from *The Washington Post*, June 13, 1979.

8. "The Decline of U.S. Power," pp. 36-41.

9. The concept of the Traders and the Prussians was first introduced by the author in "The Traders and the Prussians," *Seven Days* (March 28, 1977), pp. 32-3.

10. For discussion, see: *The Wall Street Journal*, January 21, 1980.

11. Quoted in *The New York Times*, July 19, 1980.

12. The Brown and Schlesinger statements were cited in *The New York Times*, February 26, 1979; the secret Yemen moves were disclosed in *The Washington Post*, June 3, 1979.

13. Interview, *U.S. News and World Report* (April 16, 1979), pp. 49-50.

14. Jim Hoagland i15. Quoted in "The Decline of U.S. Power," p. 88.

16. See: *The Washington Post*, June 22, 1979; and *The New York Times*, June 28, 1979.

17. Quoted in *The New York Times*, December 2, 1979.

18. *Ibid*.

19. Quoted in *The New York Times*, March 18 and July 18, 1980.

20. Quoted in *The New York Times*, May 6, 1981.

21. *Ibid*.

22. Quoted in *The New York Times*, February 4, 1981.

23. Quoted in the *San Francisco Chronicle*, March 4, 1981.

24. *Ibid*.

25. *Ibid*.

Chapter II

1. quoted in *The New York Times*, March 5, 1981.

2. Guy Pauker, *Military Implications of a Possible World Order Crisis in the 1980s*, Report no. R-2003-AF (Santa Monica: Rand Corp., 1977), pp. 1-2.

3. Harold Brown, *Department of Defense Annual Report for Fiscal Year 1981* (Washington: Department of Defense, 1980), p. 45. (Hereinafter cited as: H. Brown, *DOD Report FY81*.)

4. *Ibid*5. *Ibid*., pp. 30, 45, 61.

6. Gen. David C. Jones, *United States Military Posture for Fiscal Year 1982* (Washington: Department of Defense, 1981), p. i. (Hereinafter cited as D.C. Jones, *U.S. Military Posture FY82*.)

7. Interview in *Time* (March 16, 1981), p. 25.

8. The concept of the "Brown Doctrine" was first advanced by the author in: "The Brown Doctrine: Have R.D.F., Will Travel," *The Nation* (March 8, 1980), pp. 257, 263-6.

9. H. Brown, *DOD Report FY81*, p. 26.

10. *Ibid*., p. 10.

11. *Ibid*., p. 62.

12. *Ibid*., p. 23.

13. Maxwell D. Taylor, *The Uncertain Trumpet* (New York: Harper & Row, 1960), pp. 5-6.

14. U.S. Congress, Senate, Committee on Foreign Relations, *The Foreign Aid Program*, Compilation of Studies and Surveys, 85th Cong., 1st Sess., 1957, p. 18.

15. Rockefeller Brothers Fund, *Prospect for America: The Rockefeller Panel Reports* (Garden City, NY: Doubleday, 1961), pp. 111-12.   101

16. U.S. Congress, Senate, Committee on Armed Services, *Military Procurement Authorizations*, Fiscal Year 1966, Hearings, 89th Cong., 1st Sess., 1965, p. 120.

17. For discussion, see: Michael T. Klare, *War Without End: American Planning for the Next Vietnams* (New York: Knopf, 1972), pp. 142-64. See also: Berkeley Rice, *The C-5A Scandal* (Boston: Houghton Mifflin, 1971).

18. Cited in *The Washington Post*, November 27, 1979.

19. Maxwell D. Taylor, "The Legitimate Claims of National Security," *Foreign Affairs* (April, 1974), pp. 586-7.

20. Pauker, *Military Implications*, pp. 1-4.

21. Quoted in *The New York Times*, February 26, 1979.

22. "The Decline of U.S. Power," *Business Week* (March 12, 1979), pp. 36-42.

23. Quoted in *The New York Times*, December 2, 1979.

24. Harold Brown, Remarks at press briefing, The Pentagon, Washington, D.C., Feburary 26, 1979 (Department of Defense transcript).

25. H. Brown, *DOD Report FY81*, p. 61.

26. Harold Brown, Remarks at press conference, MacDill A.F.B., Fla., December 27, 1979 (Department of Defense transcript.)

27. Gen. P.X. Kelley, Remarks at press briefing, The Pentagon, Washington, D.C., June 18, 1980 (Department of Defense transcript.)

28. For discussion, see: *Aviation Week & Space Technology* (November 10, 1980), pp. 14-16, (November 17, 1980), pp. 21-2; *The Wall Street Journal*, March 5, 1981.

29. From transcript in *The New York Times*, June 6, 1980.

30. James H. Noyes, *The Clouded Lens* (Stanford, CA.: Hoover Institution, 1979), p. 95.

31. From transcript in *The New York Times*, June 6, 1980.

Chapter III

1. Quoted in *The New York Times*, January 24, 1980.

2. Quoted in *The Washington Post*, October 4, 1979.

3. Quoted in *The New York Times*, February 26, 1979.

4. Unnamed Defense Department official quoted in *The Washington Post*, February 5, 1980.

5. Quoted in *The New York Times*, March 5, 1981.

6. H. Brown, *DOD Annual Report FY81*, p. 55.

7. For discussion, see: U.S. Congress, Senate, Committee on Foreign

Relations, U.S. *Military Sales to Iran*, Staff Report, 94th Cong., 2nd Sess., 1976. See also: Michael T. Klare, "Arms and the Shah," *The Progressive* (August, 1979), pp. 14-21.

8. Quoted in *Chicago Sun-Times*, December 20, 1979. For background on the Administration's review, see: *The New York Times*, June 28, 1979.

9. Quoted in *The New York Times*, December 2, 1979.

10. Harold Brown, Remarks at MacDill A.F.B., December 27, 1979 (Department of Defense transcript).

11. Quoted in *The Washington Star*, February 1, 1980.

12. U.S. Congress, Senate, Committee on Armed Services, *Department of Defense Authorization for Appropriations for Fiscal Year 1981*, Hearings, 96th Cong., 1st Sess., vol. I, 1980, pp. 435-6. (Hereinafter cited as SASC, *DOD Authorization FY81*.)

13. *The Washington Post*, February 5, 1980; *The Wall Street Journal*, February 1, 1980; and, *The New York Times*, February 2, 1980.

14. Harold Brown, "The Persian Gulf and Southwest Asia," *Defense 80* (June, 1980), p. 6.

15. See: David R. Griffiths, "Rapid Deployment Scrutinized," *Aviation Week & Space Technology* (March 16, 1981), pp. 14-15.

16. George F. Kennan, guest editorial, *The New York Times*, February 1, 1980.

17. Keith A. Dunn, "Power Projection or Influence: Soviet Capabilities for the 1980s," *Naval War College Review* (September-October, 1980), pp. 31-47.

18. Organization of the Joint Chiefs of Staff, *United States Military Posture for FY 1982* (Washington, 1980), pp. 12-13.

19. Harold Brown, Summary of FY 1981 Defense Budget, Department of Defense press release, The Pentagon, Washington, D.C., January 28, 1980.

20. See descriptions in *The Washington Post*, February 1, 1981; and, *San Francisco Chronicle*, January 29, 1981. For a description of an earlier exercise with similar parameters, see: Michael T. Klare, "Fire Drill for the Carter Doctrine," *Mother Jones* (August, 1980), pp. 13-19.

21. Interview in *Business Week* (January 23, 1975).

22. Quoted in *Department of State Bulletin* (February 17, 1975), p. 220.

23. Interview in *U.S. News & World Report* (May 26, 1975).

24. Robèrt W. Tucker, "Oil: The Issue of American Intervention," *Commentary* (January, 1975), pp. 21-31.

25. Miles Ignotus, "Seizing Arab Oil," *Harper's* (March, 1975), pp. 45-62.

26. Robert W. Heinl, Jr., "Thinking the Unthinkable on Military

Takeover of Arab Oil Fields," *Human Events* (November 23, 1974), p. 12.

27. Arnaud de Borchgrave, "Intervention Wouldn't Work," *Newsweek* (March 31, 1975), pp. 48-9.

28. John M. Collins and Clyde R. Mark, "Petroleum Imports from the Persian Gulf: U.S. Armed Force to Ensure Supplies," Issue Brief, Congressional Research Service, Library of Congress, May 21, 1979.

29. *Ibid.*

30. James H. Noyes, *The Clouded Lens: Persian Gulf Security and U.S. Security* (Stanford, CA: Hoover Institution Press, 1979), p. 95.

31. For discussion, see: U.S. Congress, Senate, Committee on Foreign Relations, *Twenty-Fifth Meeting of the North Atlantic Assembly*, Report of the U.S. Delegation, 96th Cong., 2d Sess., 1980, pp. 259-65.

32. H. Brown, "The Persian Gulf and Southwest Asia," p. 6.

33. George F. Kennan, Guest editorial, *The New York Times*, February 1, 1980.

Chapter IV

1. This theme was first discussed by the author in "Resource Wars," *Harper's* (January, 1981), pp. 20-3.

2. "Now the Squeeze on Metals," *Business Week* (July 2, 1979), p. 46.

3. Quoted in *San Francisco Chronicle*, Sept. 18, 1980.

4. U.S. Congress, House, Committee on Interior & Insular Affairs, Subcommittee on Mines & Mining, *Nonfuel Minerals Policy Review*, Hearings, 96th Cong., 2nd Sess., 1980, Pt. III, p. 5. (Hereinafter cited as: Mining Subcommittee, *Nonfuel Minerals Policy.*)

5. *The New York Times*, December 8, 1980.

6. Interview, *Time* (March 16, 1981), p. 25; text of speech in *The New York Times*, April 26, 1981.

7. H. Brown, *DOD Report FY81*, p. 62.

8. Interview with Harold Brown, *U.S. News & World Report* (August 4, 1980), pp. 26-8.

9. Department of the Navy, Office of the Chief of Naval Operations, *U.S. Life Lines* (Washington, 1978), pp. 3, 7. (Hereinafter cited as: CNO, *U.S. Life Lines.*)

10. "Now the Squeeze on Metals," p. 46.

11. *Ibid.*, p. 52. See also: Herbert E. Meyer, "How We're Fixed for Strategic Minerals," *Fortune* (February 9, 1981), pp. 68-70.

12. "The Minerals Crisis," *Newsweek* (November 10, 1980), p. 98. See also: CNO, *U.S. Life Lines*, pp. 10-63.

13. CNO, *U.S. Life Lines*, p. 36.

14. David J. Kroft, "The Geopolitics of Non-Energy Minerals," *Air Force* (June, 1979), p. 77. See also: CNO, *U.S. Life Lines*.

15. CNO, *U.S. Life Lines*, pp. 17, 23, and 51.

16. Kroft, "Geopolitics," p. 78.

17. D.C. Jones, *U.S. Military Posture FY82*, p. 3.

18. Richard Barnet, *The Lean Years* (New York: Simon & Schuster, 1980), pp. 117-20. See also: "Now the Squeeze on Metals," p. 51.

19. Meyer, "How We're Fixed," p. 69.

20. Harry J. Gray, "The Crisis in Critical Minerals," Talk before the American Society for Metals, Chicago, November 14, 1979 (xerox copy supplied by United Technologies Corp.).

21. Quoted in *The New York Times*, March 19, 1981.

22. Meyer, "How We're Fixed," p. 68.

23. See: "Now the Squeeze on Metals," pp. 48-9.

24. For discussion, see: Daniel Volman: *A Continent Besieged* (Washington, D.C.: Institute for Policy Studies, 1980).

25. Mining Subcommittee, *Nonfuel Minerals Policy*, p. 6.

26. Quoted in *The New York Times*, March 5, 1981.

27. "Minerals Emerge as a Campaign Issue," *Aviation Week & Space Technology* (October 20, 1980), p. 115.

28. For discussion, see: Barnet, *The Lean Years*, pp. 125-7; *The Washington Post*, October 15, 1980.

29. Barnet, *The Lean Years*, p. 127.

30. Quoted in *The New York Times*, January 24, 1980.

31. CNO, *U.S. Life Lines*, p. 3.

32. *Ibid.*

33. Interview, *U.S. News & World Report* (February 5, 1979), p. 35.

34. On the *Spruance* caper, see: Michael T. Klare, "The Arms Overstock," *Harper's* (November, 1979), pp. 24-29.

35. Excerpts from 1980 Republican Party Platform, in *Aviation Week & Space Technology* (August 25, 1980), p. 9.

36. U.S. Department of Defense, *Highlights of Budget Revisions for Fiscal Years 1981 and 1982* (Washington, D.C., 1981). See also: *The Wall Street Journal*, March 5, 1981.

37. Caspar Weinberger, Statement before the House Budget Committee, Washington, D.C., March 20, 1981 (Department of Defense transcript).

38. D.C. Jones, *U.S. Military Posture FY82*, p. i.

39. Donald E. Fink, "Availability of Strategic Materials Debated," *Aviation Week & Space Technology* (May 5, 1980), pp. 42-55.

40. Quoted in *The Wall Street Journal*, March 16, 1981.

41. "The National Defense Stockpile," *Defense/80* (December, 1981), p. 23. See also: "Stockpile of Minerals Short of Goals," *Aviation Week & Space Technology* (May 5, 1980), p. 55; and, *The Wall Street Journal*, March 16, 1981.

42. See: Fink, "Availability Debated," pp. 42-4; Meyer, "How We're Fixed," pp. 68-70.

43. Quoted in Fink, "Availability Debated," p. 46.

44. *The Washington Post*, October 15, 1980.

45. Cited in Deborah M. Kyle, "U.S. Strategic Mineral Crunch Sparks Hill Interest," *Armed Forces Journal* (June, 1980), p. 14.

46. "Now the Squeeze on Metals," p. 51.

47. Quoted in William B. Hankee and Alwyn H. King, "The Role of Security Assistance in Maintaining Access to Strategic Resources," *Parameters*, The Journal of the Army War College, vol. VIII, no. 3 (September, 1978), p. 47.

Chapter V

1. Quoted in *The New York Times*, October 2, 1980.

2. *The New York Times*, October 4, 1979.

3. For discussion, see Jan Austin and Banning Garrett, "Quick Strike," *Inquiry* (July 24, 1978), pp. 12-15.

4. Quoted in *The New York Times*, February 27, 1979.

5. *The Washington Post*, June 22, 1979; *The Christian Science Monitor*, June 22, 1979.

6. James B. Agnew, "Unilateral Corps," *Army* (September, 1979), p. 30-3.

7. For discussion, see: Martin Binkin and Jeffrey Record, "Send in the Marines," *The Washington Post*, March 3, 1980; and, Maxwell D. Taylor, "But Not for a Pentagon Feud," *The Washington Post*, March 10, 1980.

8. Adm. Thomas B. Hayward, *CNO Report Fiscal Year 1981*, Military Posture & Budget of the U.S. Navy (Washington, D.C.: Dept. of the Navy, 1980), p. 10.

9. See: Hedrick Smith, "Iran is Helping U.S. to Shed Fear of Intervening Abroad," *The New York Times*, December 2, 1979.

10. Quoted in *The New York Times*, December 2, 1979.

11. *The Washington Star*, December 5 and 6, 1979; *The Washington Post*, December 6, 1979; *The New York Times*, December 6, 1979.

12. *The Wall Street Journal*, December 6, 1979.

13. Harold Brown, Press Conference, The Pentagon, December 14, 1979 (U.S. Department of Defense transcript).

14. Harold Brown, Press Conference, MacDill Air Force Base, December 27, 1979, U.S. Department of Defense Press Conference.

15. Quoted in *The New York Times*, January 24, 1980.

16. See: *The New York Times*, February 2, 7, and 29, 1980; *The Wall Street Journal*, February 1, 1980; *The Christian Science Monitor*, Feburary 4, 1980; and, *The Washington Star*, February 1, 1980.

17. See: *The Wall Street Journal*, February 1, 1980; *The Washington Post*, February 2, 1980; and *The New York Times*, February 7, 1980.

18. SASC, *DOD Authorization FY81*, Part 1, p. 441.

19. *Ibid.*, Part 5, pp. 3147-51.

20. *Atlanta Journal & Constitution*, June 28, 1980.

21. *The New York Times*, June 19, 1980; *The Washington Star*, June 19, 1980.

22. See: *The New York Times*, April 22, June 6, and August 19, 1980.

23. Jeffrey Record, "Why Plan Rapid Deployment for the Wrong Kind of Force," *The Washington Star*, February 3, 1980.

24. Gen. Paul X. Kelley, Press Briefing, The Pentagon, June 18, 1980 (U.S. Department of Defense transcript).

25. Quoted in *The Washington Post*, October 28, 1980.

26. *The Washington Post*, February 2, 1980; *The Christian Science Monitor*, May 11, 1981.

27. James R. Schlesinger, "Rapid (?) Deployment (?) Force (?)," *The New York Times*, September 24, 1980.

28. Quoted in *The New York Times*, October 2, 1980.

29. *The Washington Post*, September 28, 1980.

30. *Omaha World-Herald*, January 25, 1981.

31. U.S. Department of Defense, *Highlights of Budget Revisions for Fiscal Years 1981 and 1982* (Washington, D.C.: 1981).

32. *The New York Times*, April 25, 1981.

33. Interview, *The Miami Herald*, August 24, 1980.

34. From CMCHS brochure sent to local hospitals by the Department of Defense. See also: "M*A*S*H* 1981," *The Nation* (April 4, 1981), p. 390.

Chapter VI

1. *The New York Times*, February 21, 24, 25 and 26, March 1 and 3, 1981.

2. For background on the counterinsurgency programs of the Vietnam era, see: Douglas S. Blaufarb, *The Counterinsurgency Era* (New York: Free Press, 1977); and, Michael T. Klare, *War Without End* (New York: Knopf, 1972).

3. *Congressional Record* (December 4, 1980), p. E5223.

4. Jeane Kirkpatrick, "U.S. Security and Latin America," *Commentary* (January, 1981), pp. 29-40.

5. Interview in *The Miami Herald*, August 24, 1980.

6. *Army Times*, October 27, 1980.

7. *San Francisco Chronicle*, March 13, 1981.

8. See: David R. Griffiths, "Changes Urged to Improve Military Aid," *Aviation Week & Space Technology* (December 15, 1980), pp. 24-5.

9. See: *The Washington Post*, May 18, 1980; *San Francisco Examiner*, August 3, 1980.

10. From promotional brochure supplied by the American Defense Preparedness Association.

11. *Congressional Record* (December 4, 1980), p. E5223.

12. For discussion of U.S. counterinsurgency doctrine of the Vietnam era, see: Eqbal Ahmad, "The Theory and Practice of Counterinsurgency," *The Nation* (August 2, 1971), pp. 70-85; Blaufarb, *The Counterinsurgency Era*; Harry Eckstein, ed., *Internal War: Problems and Approaches* (New York: Free Press, 1964); David Galula, *Counterinsurgency Warfare* (New York: Praeger, 1964); John S. Pustay, *Counterinsurgency Warfare* (New York: Free Press, 1965); and, Charles Wolf, Jr., *United States Policy and the Third World* (Boston: Little, Brown, 1967).

13. Guest column, *The Washington Post*, February 12, 1981.

14. For an excellent critique of U.S. strategy in Vietnam, see: Charles Maechling, Jr., "Our Internal Defense Policy: A Reappraisal," *Foreign Service Journal* (January, 1969), as inserted in *Congressional Record* (February 25, 1969), pp. S2020-23.

15. Robert E. Osgood, *Limited War Revisited* (Boulder, CO: Westview Press, 1979), p. 68.

16. U. Alexis Johnson, "The Role of the Police in a Changing World," *Department of State Bulletin* (September 13, 1971), p. 282. See also: Michael T. Klare and Cynthia Arnson, *Supplying Repression* (Washington, D.C.: Institute for Policy Studies, 1981).

17. Quoted in *The Nation* (December 10, 1973), p. 620.

18. For discussion, see: Carol Ackroyd, *et. al.*, *The Technology of Political Control* (Harmondsworth: Penguin, 1977).

23. Richard A. Stewart, "Oman: The Next Crisis?" *U.S. Naval Institute Proceedings* (April, 1980), p. 97.

24. For discussion, see: George Hauser, "Blood on the Sahara," *The Progressive* (December, 1980), pp. 48-50.

25. For discussion, see: Daniel Volman, *A Continent Besieged* (Washington, D.C.: Institute for Policy Studies, 1980), pp. 9-15.

26. Quoted in *The New York Times*, June 3, 1981.

27. Telephone interview, November 7, 1980.

APPENDIX:

THE POWER PROJECTION GAP: A COMPARISON OF U.S. AND SOVIET LONG-RANGE INTERVENTION CAPABILITIES

It is generally assumed that overall U.S. and Soviet military capabilities are roughly comparable, with the U.S. advantage in technology balanced by a Soviet advantage in numbers. However, while there are many congruities and symmetries in the U.S.-Soviet military balance, it is not true that the Soviet military establishment *as a whole* resembles the U.S. war machine. Indeed, there are many disparities and asymmetries in the superpower balance, reflecting profound differences in history, military doctrine, political outlook, and technical proficiency. Only by recognizing these differences can we obtain an accurate picture of America's and Russia's military capabilities and thus of their relative capacity to use force as an instrument of national policy.

Nowhere, perhaps, is the disparity in U.S. and Soviet military capabilities more apparent than in the case of long-range intervention capabilities. While the United States has long maintained an elaborate and powerful interventionary apparatus, the Soviet Union has only lately acquired *any* forces of this sort, and its overall capacity in this area remains very limited indeed. Moreover, while American military doctrine explicitly envisions the use of military force to protect threatened U.S. interests in distant Third World areas, Soviet doctrine is markedly ambiguous on the potential role of Soviet forces in limited conflicts arising outside of the U.S.S.R.'s immediate sphere of influence (i.e., Eastern Europe and border states like Afghanistan and Mongolia). Thus, while there is considerable evidence that Moscow plans to acquire additional interventionary capabilities, Western analysts are uncertain as to where, and under what conditions such forces may be employed.

This is not to say that Moscow lacks the capacity or will to employ military force in the pursuit of its foreign policy objectives; indeed, recent events in Angola, Ethiopia, and Afghanistan tell us otherwise. But because Moscow has provided military aid to beleaguered allies in Africa, and has intervened to prevent the collapse of a client regime on its borders, we cannot assume that it is therefore willing and able to commit Soviet forces to a full-scale intervention of the Vietnam type *far beyond its own territory*. As we shall see, the U.S.S.R. does not presently possess such a capability, nor is it certain that recent acquisitions are intended to create one. It is, however, likely that Moscow will continue to assist friendly regimes in Africa and the Middle East, thus prompting calls for U.S. counteraction—including, perhaps, direct military intervention—to deter such Soviet ventures. And given the danger that precipitous U.S. action could trigger a major conflict, it is essential that we appreciate the relative imbalance between U.S. and Soviet intervention capabilities, and thus the inherent limits to Soviet adventurism abroad.

In this essay, we will compare the long-range intervention capabilities of the two superpowers, and examine the military doctrine which governs their design and deployment. Before proceeding to this study, however, it is necessary to say a few words about nomenclature. By *long-range intervention capabilities*, we mean those military forces created by a country for the purpose of invading and occupying distant countries in order to affect their political behavior. In Pentagon parlance, such capabilities are called "projection forces" (as in the "projection of power"), and are characterized by their capacity "for long-distance, forcible insertion into enemy-occupied territory against armed opposition."[1] Normally, such forces are assumed to include both ground combat units plus the air- and sea-transport capabilities used to carry them to the battlefield. Projection forces may of course be used for other purposes—to intimidate   111 hostile powers through "show of force" operations; to assist allied governments under attack from a common enemy; or to reinforce regular military forces during a major war—but it is their capacity to *forcibly occupy enemy-held territory far beyond a country's normal defense perimeter* which distinguishes interventionary forces from other conventional military forces.

(To prevent misunderstanding, let it be said that we are not talking here about interventionary *acts.* Clearly, any steps taken by one country to effect political developments in another country—including the sale or delivery of arms, deployments of military "advisers" or technicians, covert intelligence operations, economic "destabilization" measures, etc.—can be termed interventionary. By interventionary *forces,* however, we mean only those units which are capable of using military power for such purposes against armed resistance. Needless to say, it is the very *existence* of such forces—i.e., the shared perception that they can be called in as the last resort—which often underlies the effectiveness of lesser measures.)

Having made these distinctions, we can turn to an examination of U.S. and then Soviet intervention capabilities. In each case, we will begin with a review of the doctrines and strategies which govern the size, structure, and operational deployment of these forces.

The One-and-a-Half War Doctrine

Ever since the end of World War II, the United States has pursued a "forward-deployed" strategy whereby large numbers of troops are based overseas in order to secure the boundaries of the Western world. Most of these troops are stationed along the principal East-West frontiers in Europe and along the 38th parallel in Korea, but another set of forces has always been reserved for contingencies arising elsewhere. These latter forces, based in the United States, at sea, and at key bases abroad, are on permanent call for deployment to distant troublespots at the discretion of the President. Although trained and equipped for forcible insertion into enemy-held territory, these "projection" forces have also been used in a threatening mode, to signal Washington's capacity to commence hostilities if an errant government fails to alter its objectional behavior.*

U.S. projection forces also constitute part of the nation's stand-by reserve for meeting the "half war" requirement in the Pentagon's "one-and-a-half-war" planning model. Under current doctrine, U.S. war planners assume that America may someday have to fight a major war in Europe against Warsaw Pact forces (one war) and, *at the same time,* a limited conflict elsewhere (the half war). In order to guarantee that Washington can respond to a minor contingency in the Third World without in any way diminishing its capacity to withstand the Russians in Europe, the one-and-a-half war strategy requires the maintenance of powerful combat forces *extraneous* to the NATO military establishment.[3] (Some analysts believe that the Reagan Administration is moving toward a "two-and-a-half war" doctrine, requiring the development of forces for a full-war capability in the Persian Gulf.)

This concept of a "half war" scenario reflects Washington's conviction that the U.S. national security is threatened as much by political and economic turbulence in the Third World as by a hypothetical East-West war in Europe. Because the U.S. economy is becoming increasingly dependent on foreign sources of raw materials—particularly energy sources—as well as on overseas markets for U.S. manufactured goods, America's "vital interests" are now seen as including unimpeded access to overseas markets and materials as well as control over the world's key maritime trade routes. "The United States has become irreversibly involved in world issues," then Secretary of Defense Harold Brown told Congress on January 25, 1979. "Our economy has come to depend heavily on imports of energy supplies and raw materials, and nine percent of our GNP now results from the sale of U.S. goods and services abroad." To protect these interests, and to ensure the survival of pro-U.S. governments abroad, "we are bound to

---

*"The protection of U.S. interests," former chairman of the Joint Chiefs of Staff General George S. Brown told Congress in 1978, "may require the availability and possible use of U.S. military forces in areas where instability, increased tension, or overt conflict affect those interests. Experience since World War II indicates that the timely use of military forces for demonstration or show of force has sometimes been sufficient to prevent open hostilities. On the other hand, the deployment and use of relatively larger forces may be required."[2]

have a strategic stake in such distant places as the Sea of Japan, the Strait of Malacca, the Persian Gulf, the Dardanelles, the Baltic, and the Barents Sea."[4] When U.S. access to these strategic areas is jeopardized, Brown declared a year later, we must be prepared "to move forces of appropriate size quickly over great distances to deter or, if necessary to defeat threats to our vital interests."[5]

Following the Vietnam war, some U.S. leaders argued that America should avoid the use of military force in future Third World conflicts. "The lesson [of Vietnam]," Senator Edward Kennedy told the Senate during a historic 1975 Senate debate on U.S. foreign policy, "is that we must throw off the cumbersome mantle of world policeman." And Senator Alan Cranston declared: "The United States should be a peaceful world neighbor instead of a militant world meddler."[6] Such views clearly influenced the 1975 Congressional decision to block U.S. military involvement in Angola. But growing concern about America's dependence on imported oil, coupled with recent developments in the Middle East and what is perceived as a more activist Soviet foreign policy, has a renewed commitment to intervention as a final resort of U.S. foreign policy. This stance was formally enunciated in President Carter's 1980 State of the Union address, when he declared that any attempt to block U.S. access to Persian Gulf oil "will be regarded as an assault on the vital interests of the United States," and would therefore "be repelled by any means necessary, including military force."[7]

To implement this policy, popularly known as the "Carter Doctrine," the Department of Defense launched a major effort to expand U.S. interventionary capabilities. First and foremost among these initiatives was the creation of the Rapid Deployment Force (RDF), a 200,000-man assault force based in the United States and available for rapid deployment to remote Third World battlefields. To ensure that the RDF can be quickly transported to distant troublespots and then adequately supported in battle, the Pentagon also announced plans to expand U.S. air- and sealift capabilities, and to establish new basing facilities in the Persian Gulf/Indian Ocean area. Insisting that even these ambitious plans are insufficient to protect U.S. interests in the Gulf area, President Reagan has called for still further additions to the U.S. interventionary apparatus, including

114

the acquisitions of several more aircraft carriers and other air and naval support forces (see details, below).

While protection of the oil flow from the Middle East remains the principal rationale for expansion of America's interventionary capabilities, other threats have also been cited to justify such measures. Arguing that U.S. security and prosperity is threatened by what he called "international turbulence"—meaning social, political, and economic disorder in the Third World—Defense Secretary Brown advocated a more vigorous U.S. effort in combatting hijackings, hostage-takings, guerrilla raids, and similar provocations. "In a world of disputes and violence," he affirmed in 1980, "we cannot afford to go abroad unarmed."[8] This outlook is fully shared by President Reagan, who warned on January 27, 1981, that he would order "swift and effective retribution" against terrorists who attack American diplomats abroad.[9] The Reagan Administration has also vowed to support pro-U.S. regimes threatened by insurgent attack—especially if the rebels are receiving Soviet or Cuban arms and assistance. Thus, when the U.S.-backed junta in El Salvador came under assault by revolutionary guerrillas, Reagan authorized a massive increase in military aid and approved the deployment of several dozen combat advisers. All this suggests that the current buildup of conventional military forces such as those committed to the RDF will be accompanied by the expansion of "unconventional warfare" forces—the Army's Special Forces (the "Green Berets"), the Air Force's Special Operations Force (SOF), and the Navy's SEAL (Sea/Air/Land) commandos—and other specialized interventionary forces.

U.S. Interventionary Forces

For planning and budgetary purposes, the U.S. projection capability is assumed by the Department of Defense to be constituted of the following combat, transport, and supply elements:

● *The U.S. Marine Corps,* consisting of three Marine divisions of 20,000 men each and their associated Marine Air Wings. Considered the interventionary force *par excellence,* the Marine Corps now numbers 192,000 men and   115 women, with an additional 30,000 (representing one division plus one air wing) held in the Reserve. Marine assets include 364 combat aircraft (F-4s, AV-8s, A-4s, and A-6s), 438 helicopters (includes 54 AH-1J gunships), 575 M-60 tanks, and assorted artillery pieces. Normally, one Marine Amphibious Unit (a reinforced battalion assault team plus associated landing ships) is stationed in the Mediterranean and two in the Pacific.[10] The Marine Corps is also expected to play a major role in the newly-activated Rapid Deployment Force, with three amphibious brigades—each of about 16,000 troops—committed to the RDF lineup.[11]

● *U.S. Army mobile strike forces*, encompassing the 15,000-man 82nd Airborne Division, and the 18,000-strong 101st Air Assault division, the Special Forces ("Green Berets"), and the Rangers. These units, normally based in the United States (the 82nd at Fort Bragg, N.C., and the 101st at Fort Campbell, Ky.), are kept at a high state of readiness for deployment on short notice to troublespots abroad. All these forces, moreover, are committed to the RDF force structure. The 82nd Division lacks an integral air arm, but the 101st Division maintains 480 helicopters in its inventory; both divisions, moreover, are normally accompanied by several Tactical Air Command wings of 75-100 planes each in major deployments abroad. In the event of a major crisis, the 82nd and 101st divisions could also be reinforced by one or both of two Army infantry divisions held in the United States for non-NATO contingencies.[12] For *lesser* contingencies, on the other hand, Washington can employ such airborne units as the Army Special Forces, the Rangers, and the elite "Delta Team" anti-terrorist force (the unit that was used in the abortive effort to rescue U.S. hostages in Iran.)[13]

● *U.S. Air Force transport capabilities*, now consisting of 70 C-5A *Galaxy* heavy transports, 234 C-141 *Starlifter* medium transports, and 234 C-130 *Hercules* tactical transports. These are the planes which would be used to transport Army and/or Marine units to the battlefield in any future interventions abroad. All told, The C-5As and C-141s can carry 16,000 tons of cargo or 60,000 fully-equipped soldiers over distances of 3,000 miles or more, while the C-130s can carry 5,125 tons or 21,500 troops over 2,500 miles.[14] The C-141s are now being "stretched" by the addition of an extended fuselage section, thereby

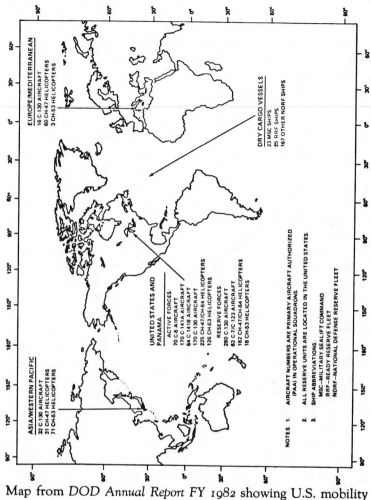

EUROPE/MEDITERRANEAN
16 C-130 AIRCRAFT
60 CH-47 HELICOPTERS
3 CH-53 HELICOPTERS

DRY CARGO VESSELS
23 MSC SHIPS
25 RRF SHIPS
167 OTHER NDRF SHIPS

UNITED STATES AND
PANAMA
ACTIVE FORCES:
70 C-5 AIRCRAFT
170 C-141A AIRCRAFT
64 C-141B AIRCRAFT
170 C-130 AIRCRAFT
225 CH-47/CH-54 HELICOPTERS
126 CH-53 HELICOPTERS

RESERVE FORCES:
280 C-130 AIRCRAFT
62 C-7/C-123 AIRCRAFT
182 CH-47/CH-54 HELICOPTERS
18 CH-53 HELICOPTERS

ASIA/WESTERN PACIFIC
32 C-130 AIRCRAFT
31 CH-47 HELICOPTERS
71 CH-53 HELICOPTERS

NOTES 1. AIRCRAFT NUMBERS ARE PRIMARY AIRCRAFT AUTHORIZED
(PAA) IN OPERATIONAL SQUADRONS.

2. ALL RESERVE UNITS ARE LOCATED IN THE UNITED STATES.

3. SHIP ABBREVIATIONS:
MSC—MILITARY SEALIFT COMMAND
RRF—READY RESERVE FLEET
NDRF—NATIONAL DEFENSE RESERVE FLEET

Map from *DOD Annual Report FY 1982* showing U.S. mobility assets.

expanding U.S. airlift capabilities without increasing the quantity of aircraft (according to the Air Force, the "stretch program will add the equivalent of 90 C-141s to the U.S. airlift fleet). The Pentagon is also planning to buy several dozen McDonnell-Douglas KC-10A cargo/tanker planes to enhance the range of the U.S. airlift fleet, and to acquire 100 or more C-X intercontinental transport planes for an estimated $6 billion. (As of August 1981, the Air Force had not fully established the specifications for the proposed 117

C-X and it is still not certain when and if Congress will approve funding for the controversial aircraft.[15]) The Pentagon's transport capability can also be augmented on short notice by the 385 commercial transports (727s, 747s, etc.) in the Civil Reserve Air Fleet (CRAF).

● *U.S. Navy carrier forces*, consisting of thirteen carriers and their aircraft, plus associated escort and supply vessels. These forces, which can be brought to bear against any overseas power without reliance on foreign bases, are rightfully considered the backbone of America's power projection capability.* All told, the existing carrier force can deploy an estimated 800 fighters and ground-support aircraft (F-14s, F-4s, A-7s, A-6s) plus assorted ASW (antisubmarine warfare) and reconnaissance planes and helicopters.[16] In line with the "Carter Doctrine" and U.S. plans to protect the oil flow from the Persian Gulf, President Reagan has pledged to expand the carrier fleet in order to ensure a permanent carrier presence in the Indian Ocean area. Funds for a new nuclear-powered carrier were requested in the Fiscal 1982 budget, and it is likely that one or two more will be funded in the succeeding four years, bringing the total carrier force to 15 to 16 vessels by the late 1980s.[17]

● *Air Force tactical airpower*, provided by the 1,692 fighters and attack planes (F-4s, F-15s, F-16s, and A-10s) of the Tactical Air Command (TAC). These aircraft are organized into 26 active wings of three squadrons each (another 11 wings, with 822 fighters, are in reserve), and are supported by several hundred reconnaissance, electronic warfare, and observation planes.[18] These forces, according to the Joint Chiefs of Staff (JCS), "have the potential to rapidly concentrate and apply military power anywhere in the world." Because many TAC aircraft are forward-based in Europe (29 fighter squadrons) and the Western Pacific (9 fighter squadrons), and because they can be flown rapidly and without intermediate stopovers (all TAC aircraft are air-refuelable) to distant troublespots, these forces are considered "especially crucial in the early stages of conventional conflict, before ground and sea-

---

*It is important to note, however, that these forces would also be expected to play a major role in any future conflict in Western Europe or Korea, in which case they would be unavailable for lesser contingencies arising in the Third World.

based forces have been deployed or reinforced."[19] Four TAC fighter/attack wings have been committed to the RDF, along with several reconnaissance squadrons, a wing of Boeing E-3A radar patrol planes, and a wing of B-52 intercontinental bombers armed with conventional munitions.[20]

● *U.S. Navy amphibious lift*, now provided by 64 amphibious assault and transport vessels. This total includes two LCC amphibious command ships, five LHA helicopter assault ships, seven LPH amphibious assault ships, five LKA amphibious cargo ships, fourteen LPD amphibious transport docks, thirteen LSD dock landing ships, and twenty LST tank landing ships. All told, these vessels carry the equivalent of one Marine division with all of its combat equipment, and can deliver this force directly to the battlefield using their self-contained fleet of some 300 helicopters and 100 landing barges.[21] To enhance this capability (and to replace older vessels), the Navy plans to acquire a fleet of new dock-landing ships (the LSD-41 class) and helicopter assault ships (the proposed LHDX). (One LSD-41 was funded in Fiscal 1981 and two more requested in 1982.) Furthermore, to provide the Rapid Deployment Force with additional sealift support, the Pentagon is buying eight SL-7 container ships which will be remodeled in a "ro/ro" (roll-on/roll-off) configuration for rapid loading and unloading, along with a flotilla of twelve "Maritime Prepositioning Ships" (MPS) which will be loaded with military gear and "pre-positioned" at friendly ports near potential conflict zones.[22]

All this represents but the "cutting edge" of the U.S. power projection capability. A full accounting of this force would have to include the Strategic Air Command tankers used for in-flight refueling of combat and transport aircraft, the "underway replenishment" ships used for at-sea resupply of naval vessels, and a global network of communications, logistics, and intelligence-gathering facilities. In its entirety, the U.S. power projection capability probably involves some 750,000 uniformed personnel—about 35 percent of total Armed Forces manpower—and consumes one-third or more of the total Pentagon budget.[23]

For some U.S. strategists, even this prodigious force is insufficient to protect all U.S. interests abroad. Arguing that existing air- and sea lift capabilities are woefully inadequate to move substantial U.S. forces to the Persian Gulf in enough time to stave off a hypothetical Soviet invasion, Defense Secretary Weinberger has called for a further expansion of military transport resources, and has proposed the basing of some U.S. forces in the Gulf area itself. "We must have a presence in the region," he told the House Armed Services Committee on March 4, 1981, "and there must be facilities there that we can use to make our presence credible."[24] Weinberger has also called for the reactivation of two World War II battleships—the *Iowa* and the *New Jersey*—plus the reactivation of the 30-year-old aircraft carrier *Oriskany*. The U.S. power projection capability will also benefit from other initiatives proposed by the Reagan Administration, including an across-the-board expansion in tactical air forces and surface naval forces.[25] If, as is likely, these initiatives are endorsed by Congress, overall U.S. interventionary capabilities will be significantly superior to those described above by the end of this decade.

Soviet Military Doctrine

Turning now to the Russians, we find a somewhat different set of strategic priorities. While U.S. military doctrine emphasizes a "forward defense" at the outer boundaries of the Western world—Germany, Turkey, Korea, etc.— Soviet doctrine stresses the fortification of the U.S.S.R. itself as an impregnable bulwark against Western attack. Thus, while nearly half of all the U.S. ground combat units are statined overseas, at least 80 percent of Soviet divisions are based in the U.S.S.R. itself with the remainder stationed in Eastern Europe (viewed at the "gateway" to Moscow) and in the border state of Afghanistan.[26] Given the grim experience of World War II—in which perhaps 20 million Soviets lost their lives—defense of the Motherland is quite naturally seen as the overriding mission of the Soviet military establishment. This view is reinforced by Moscow's belief that the U.S.S.R. constitutes both the supreme achievement and the ultimate guardian of Socialist society; in any war with the West, therefore, Soviet forces will be fighting not only to defend their homeland but also to ensure the survival of Socialism itself. Nationalism and ideology thus combined to perpetuate the "siege mentality" which governs the disposition of Soviet military forces.[27]

Soviet military theory also deviates from American doctrine in prescribing the types of war which Soviet forces must be prepared to fight. Whereas U.S. doctrine holds that American forces must be highly diversified in order to handle a wide spectrum of possible conflict situations—ranging from a limited counterinsurgency operation to a full-scale nuclear war—Soviet doctrine assumes that any East-West clash will automatically escalate to a full-scale war and that all Soviet forces must therefore be designed with this contingency in mind. Thus, while the United States maintains both "heavy" divisions for a European contingency and "light" divisions for a Third World contingency, almost all Soviet divisions are designed for a full-scale engagement with the West.[28]

If follows from all this that there is no equivalent, in Soviet doctrine, of America's "one-and-a-half war" strategy. In contrast to the U.S. practice of reserving a large bloc of forces for a "half war" contingency in the Third World, the overwhelming bulk of Soviet forces are committed to a strategic defense role. And while Soviet doctrine distinguishes between all-out nuclear war and limited conflicts, it is extremely ambiguous regarding Soviet participation in the latter—which are assumed, in official texts, to involve a clash between the Western powers and radical Third World regimes. The few Soviet statements on this question indicate merely that the U.S.S.R. is prepared to provide unspecified but limited military support to friendly countries under assault by the West.[29] Nevertheless, as Moscow's ties with radical Thrid World governments have expanded, so has its apparent commitment to help defend such regimes against hostile forces. For the most part, Soviet action has been confined to accessory functions: the delivery of arms and technical assistance; naval action designed to deter Western intervention; and, in the case of Angola and Ethiopia, logistical support for Cuban expeditionary forces.[30] Only in Afthanistan has Moscow committed its own forces in a direct interventionary role.

In the wake of Afghanistan, many Western analysts have argued that Moscow is now prepared to mount a full-scale intervention of the Vietnam type in distant Third World locales. Other experts suggest, however, that Afghanistan cannot necessarily be considered a precedent for such action becasue that country shares a common border with   121 the U.S.S.R. and has long been viewed in Moscow as a buffer against hostile nations to the South. "The official American interpretation of what happened in Afghanistan," former diplomat George Kennan wrote in *The New York Times*, neglects such factors as "geographic proximity... and political instability in what is, after all, a border country of the Soviet Union." Such factors do not justify the Soviet invasion, Kennan argued, but they do suggest "defensive rather than offensive factors."[31] Such an interpretation would be consistent, moreover, with Soviet doctrinal statements defining limited wars as a Western/Third World conflict involving, at most, a limited Soviet backup role.[32]

Although Western analysts tend to discount the relevance of Soviet military theory (except when seeking evidence for their own interpretations of Soviet behavior), the evidence suggests that the Russians—no less than the Americans—tend to design and deploy their forces in accordance with established military doctrine. While America's "one-and-a-half-war" strategy has resulted in the creation of a substantial pool of forces designed for a Third World contingency, Soviet forces are principally designed for an all-out war with the West, and, to a lesser extend, with the Peoples Republic of China. Nevertheless, growing Soviet emphasis on the defense of friendly Third World regimes has apparently led to the expansion of selected military capabilities, including air- and sealift forces (to provide logistical support) and naval forces (to protect Soviet supply convoys and to discourage Western intervention). As Moscow expands its ties with Third World regimes, therefore, we will undoubtedly see a further expansion of these and related capabilities.

Soviet Interventionary Capabilities

While there is no Soviet equivalent to America's "one-and-a-half war" planning model, some Soviet central-war forces exhibit characteristics comparable to U.S. projection forces and would, presumably, perform a similar role should the U.S.S.R. engage in intervention-type operations overseas. These forces are:

● *Soviet Naval Infantry*, a small force of 12,000

"marines" assigned to Soviet fleets and river flotillas. This modest force of five regiments was created in the early 1960s to provide the Soviet Navy with a limited amphibious assault capability. Each of these regiments incorporates an armored battalion with some 30 light tanks; unlike the U.S. Marines, however, the Naval Infantry does not possess an integral air arm. According to former Pentagon analyst Graham Turbiville, the principal mission of the Naval Infantry is to secure the coastal flanks of Warsaw Pact ground formations in Europe—where Soviet land-based aircraft would be available to provide the necessary air cover.[33] (Normally, the Naval Infantry carries only 4 to 5 days' worth of combat supplies, and in Warsaw Pact exercises is immediately replaced by regular ground troops after their particular objective has been seized.[34]) Theoretically, these forces could also be used in a seaborne attack outside of the European theater, but their small size and lack of organic airpower and "staying power" would place them at a severe disadvantage in any assaults on heavily defended positions. As Michael MccGwire noted in *Soviet Naval Developments*, "the gradual build-up and present size" of these forces "do not support the theory that the reactivation of the Naval Infantry in 1963 signalled a Soviet intention to develop a Western-style overseas intervintion capability."[35] However, the appearance of the *Ivan Rogov* amphibious landing ship (see below) in the Indian Ocean and other foreign waters suggests that Moscow may contemplate use of the Naval Infantry for limited assault missions such as port seizures (for the supply of allied forces) or for emergency evacuation of Soviet personnel.

● *Soviet airborne forces*, consisting of seven paratroop divisions of about 7,500 men each equipped with infantry arms, antitank missiles, and mobile artillery. (An eighth division is used for training.) Although often compared to the U.S. 82nd and 101st divisions, Soviet paratroop forces do not seem to have a primary Third World orientation but rather appear designed for a support role in the European theater. Thus, in recent Warsaw Pact training exercises, they have been used to neutralize enemy strong-points in front of the main ground assault, and to occupy ports, airstrips, bridges, and the like behind enemy lines.[36] In 1979, however, some of these units were used to inaugurate the Soviet intervention in Afghanistan, and it is possible that they would also be used to suppress future anti-Soviet uprisings within Eastern Europe or, conceivably, to reinforce beleaguered Soviet allies in Africa and other Third World locales. If deployed overseas, however, these lightly-armed assault forces would be at a severe disadvantage in any conflict with a sophisticated, well-equipped adversary. As noted by the Joint Chiefs of Staff in their Fiscal 1982 assessment of Soviet capabilities, "The effectiveness of Soviet airborne forces in conflicts far from the U.S.S.R. .... would be hampered by the limitations of Soviet long-range airlift and the lack of immediately available tactical air forces."[37]

● *Soviet air transport capabilities*, now encompassing the 1,200 transport planes assigned to the Military Transport Aviation (VTA) service. The long-range component of the fleet presently consists of 560 An-12 medium transports, some 50 An-22 heavy cargo planes, and 80-100 Il-76 jet transports. (The VTA fleet can also be augmented by the considerable resources of Aeroflot, the Soviet airline, just as U.S. military transports can be augmented by civilian airliners in the Civil Reserve Air Fleet.) The VTA transports are capable of moving a significant quantity of troops and materiel over moderate distances, but lack the airborne refueling capability of America's C-5A transports and thus must land at friendly airports for refueling on long-haul operations. Also, the largest of these aircraft, the An-22 turboprop, can carry only 175,000 pounds of cargo compared to the C-5A's 220,000 pounds, and has a shorter operating range (3,100 miles compared to 3,750 miles).[38] (Some analysts believe that that Russians are working on a replacement for the An-22, which was last produced in 1974, but no details of such an aircraft have yet been disclosed.) And while these aircraft could be used to supply Soviet forces in the event of a major operation abroad (as indeed they have been used in Angola, Ethiopia, and Afghanistan), they could only be employed in the absence of an enemy air threat since the Russians lack carrier-based fighters to protect its unarmed transports.

● *Soviet carrier forces*, presently consisting of two *Moskva*-class helicopter carriers and two *Kiev*-class helicopter/ VTOL (vertical-take-off-and-landing planes) carriers with two more *Kiev*-class vessels under construction. Although often equated with American carriers, these Russian vessels are in no way comparable to U.S. attack carriers with their dozens of high-performance combat planes. The 15,000-ton *Moskva*, and her sister ship *Leningrad*, can only carry a dozen or so KA-25 ASW (anti-submarine warfare) helicopters armed with depth charges and torpedoes, while the 40,000-ton *Kiev*, and sister *Minsk*, carry 25 KA-25s plus a dozen or so Yak-36 VTOL combat planes.[39] (The Yak-36 has rarely carried external munitions during operational flights from the *Kiev* or *Minsk*, so its ultimate combat role is still unknown; because of weight restrictions, however, they are not believed to have a significant offensive capability.) The Soviets call their carriers "anti-submarine cruisers," and everything we know about them to date suggests that their principal wartime function is to locate, track, and destroy American missile-carrying submarines (and, by inference, to defend Soviet missile subs against U.S. attack subs).[40] Recent naval exercises involving both the *Minsk* and the *Ivan Rogov* suggest that Moscow may contemplate using carrier-based helicopters to lift Naval Infantry forces in limited assault missions, but given the lack of supporting air cover such operations would necessarily be limited to attacks on relatively undefended positions. The Soviets are also reportedly building a genuine aircraft carrier equipped with catapults for launching combat planes, but preliminary observation suggests that the new vessel—presumably due to enter operational service in the late 1980s—will only be half the size of current U.S. carriers like the *Nimitz*.[41]

● *Soviet tactical airpower*, provided by the 4,300 combat planes of Soviet Frontal Aviation (FA). While recent Soviet fighters (MiG-23, MiG-25, MiG-27, Su-17, Su-24) have proven far more capable than earlier models, the FA inventory continues to include large numbers of less-capable MiG-21s, Su-7s, and Yak-28s.[42] Moreover, Soviet tactical aircraft generally have a smaller combat radius than their American counterparts, and lack an in-flight refueling capability. These limitations, according to Keith Dunn of the U.S. Army War College, "make it difficult for the U.S.S.R. to redeploy its FA assets rapidly over long distances."[43] In Afghanistan, of course, Soviet aircraft were able to fly combat missions from bases inside Soviet territory; on those occasions when Moscow has provided fighters to allies elsewhere, however, it has usually had to move them by ship.[44]

● *Soviet amphibious lift*, now provided by some 88 amphibious cargo ships, of which only 28 (14 *Alligator*-class LSTs, 13 *Ropucha*-class LSTs, and the new *Ivan Rogov*) are considered capable of "open-ocean transit" by the Department of Defense.[45] Most Soviet amphibious vessels are much smaller than their American counterparts—the 5,800-ton *Alligator* types, for instance, have less than one-third the lift capacity of the comparable U.S. *Iwo Jima*-class transports—and they lack a self-contained helicopter off-load capability.[46] Even the new *Ivan Rogov*, at 13,000 tons the largest Soviet amphibious vessel, is considered a "far cry" from the 39,000-ton U.S. *Tarawa*-class helicopter assault ship.[47] Although some Soviet amphibious vessels have joined combat ships on voyages to the Indian Ocean and the Pacific, Siegfried Breyer and Norman Polmar note in their *Guide to the Soviet Navy* that "these amphibious forces are primarily maintained to support ground and naval operations along the Soviet periphery."[48] Some analysts have suggested, however, that the appearance of the *Ivan Rogov* (which is expected to be the first of several vessels of this class) signals a new Soviet drive to expand its overseas amphibious assault capability.

As in the case of U.S. projection forces, any full accounting of Soviet capabilities would have to include other military assets, including the bombers and tankers of the Long-Range Air Force (the Soviet equivalent of the U.S. Strategic Air Command), naval support ships and intelligence-collection vessels, and shore-based naval aircraft. Together, these forces provide the U.S.S.R. with a substantial capacity for aiding friendly forces abroad or for intervention on the Soviet periphery—but only a modest capacity for long-range intervention against well-armed opponents elsewhere. As the Joint Chiefs of Staff noted in 1981, "the Soviets . . . now have the capability to deploy forces that could be highly effective against *light or disorganized opposition*," but would be at a severe disadvantage in combat "against heavy oposition."[49] (Emphasis added.) In any major undertaking, of course, Soviet projecton forces could be reinforced by regular combat units—

but this would require the diversion of forces committed to either the European or Siberian theater (since, as we have seen, the Soviets do not have an independent troop reserve such as that mandated by the U.S. "one-and-a-half war" strategy), and thus is not likely to be considered except in this extraordinary (and, at this point, unforeseen) circumstances.

Some Western analysts believe that Moscow has embarked upon an ambitious effort to overcome the deficiencies in its power projection capabilities. The appearance of the *Ivan Rogov*, for instance, has been cited as evidence of a Soviet drive to acquire a high-seas amphibious fleet such as that long possessed by the United States. But while some modernization and expansion programs may indeed be underway, there is as yet no evidence of a massive Soviet effort to duplicate U.S. power projection forces. The Naval Infantry and the Airborne force have grown only slightly over the past ten years, and the VTA and Amphibious fleets are not being expanded at anything near the rate that would be necessary to catch up with U.S. capabilities in this area.[50] What we are probably witnessing, instead, is a continuing Soviet effort to replace obsolete and low-performance equipment with more modern and capable hardware. Thus old propeller-driven An-12 transports are being replaced by the jet-powered Il-76, but the *overall* size of the VTA fleet has actually diminished (from 1,700 aircraft in 1974 to 1,300 today[51]) because older planes are being retired faster than new planes are being built.

Undoubtedly, there are some Soviet officers who, like their American counterparts, believe that their country's projection capabilities are inadequate for many of the likely contingencies they face in the years ahead. Certainly the U.S.S.R.'s growing involvement in Africa and Afghanistan may generate new requirements for projection-type forces; at the same time, it is also possible that the rising cost of such ventures, coupled with the high risk of failure (especially in Afghanistan), may prompt Moscow to reduce its commitment to such undertakings. It is also possible that, in the face of the massive military buildup ordered by President Reagan, the Soviets will revert to a more defensive posture, emphasizing the security of Mother Russia and immediately adjacent "buffer" states like Poland. For these reasons, considerable caution should be exercised in postulating elaborate Soviet plans for an expanded long-range interventionary capacity.

The Final Score:
A Comparison of U.S. & Soviet Projection Capabilities

Having examined the principal components of the U.S. and Soviet intervention capabilities, it is time to draw some conclusions about their relative strength and effectiveness. First, we can add up the numbers involved in order to obtain some rough indicators of relative capacity:

● *Manpower*: counting "marines" and air-mobile forces only, we have 215,000 for the U.S. and 72,000 for the U.S.S.R., giving the U.S. a 3:1 advantage.

● *Carrier forces*: In numbers of vessels, the U.S. has the advantage with 13 carriers compared to 4 for the Soviets. (In terms of *displacement*, U.S. carriers weigh in at 1,039,600 tons, compared to 114,000 tons for the U.S.S.R.: a 9:1 advantage.) U.S. carriers can launch 800 attack aircraft compared to perhaps 40 Yak-36s of questionable value (a 20:1 advantage, which probably expands to about 100:1 when U.S. advantages in range and payload are factored in).

● *Airlift*: U.S. transports (C-5As, C-141s, C-130s) can together deliver 21,135 tons while Soviet transports (An-12s, An-22s, and Il-76s) can deliver 24,140 tons; this slight advantage for the Soviets is offset, however, by the superior range and in-flight refuel capacity of U.S. transports.

● *Amphibious lift*: the total displacement of U.S. amphibious vessels is 944,000 tons, compared to 175,000 tons for Soviet vessels, giving the U.S. a 5:1 advantage.

These figures clearly indicate that in most basic categories U.S. projection forces are considerably superior to those possessed by the Soviet Union. Indeed, it could be said that Moscow suffers from a severe "power projection gap" vis-a-vis the United States. America's numerical lead is enhanced, moreover, by significant U.S. advantages in the performance capabilities of these forces. Thus Soviet transport planes lack the in-flight refueling capacity of U.S. transports, Soviet amphibious vessels lack an integral helicopter lift capability, and Soviet marines and airborne forces lack the integral air support and logistical "staying power" of their American counterparts. Moreover, Moscow's long-range command, control, and communications facilities (in Pentagon parlance, C^3 or "C-cubed" systems) are also inferior to comparable American systems and Soviet forces lack the "portable battle staff" capability provided by the Air Force's E-3A AWACS (Airborne Warning and Control System) aircraft.[52]

More important than any of these disadvantages, however, is the U.S.S.R.'s lack of any true attack carriers: without assured air superiority over the battlefield, Soviet assault forces would be highly vulnerable to enemy air and armored forces in any encounter with a strong opponent. This deficiency may be corrected in the 1990s if, as reported by the Joint Chiefs of Staff in their 1982 posture statement, Moscow intends to build an attack carrier of the American type. For the present, however, "the lack of sea-based tactical air support greatly limits Soviet ability to carry out amphibious landings against heavy opposition."[53]

Aside from these material deficiencies, the U.S.S.R.'s power projection capability also suffers from the *doctrinal rigidity* of Soviet military thinking. While the United States has long maintained highly-mobile strike forces for the long-range projection function, the Soviet Union has structured almost all of its forces for high-intensity conflict in the European and Siberian theaters, and therefore lacks a sizeable pool of assault forces for use in other sorts of conflicts elsewhere. This handicap is compounded by the fact that Soviet main-force units are tank- and vehicle-heavy and thus cannot be easily or quickly redeployed to other locations. As noted by Keith Dunn of the Army War College, Soviet war plans which call for "a preponderance of armored/mechanized forces" may be appropriate "for a certain type of Eurasian land battle, but they inherently make ground divisions less 'projectable.'"[54] And because their training and tactical doctrine is optimized for high-speed mechanized operations, these units often find themselves at a disadvantage when actually employed against insurgent or irregular forces in a Third World environment. "Soviet forces stress mobility, and Soviet troops are trained to fight from armored vehicles until forced to dismount," the Joint Chiefs of Staff noted recently. "However appropriate these tactics are for war in Europe, they are not optimum for conditions in Afghanistan," where "the rugged terrain is not suitable for wheeled or tracked vehicles, and [where] resistance fighters are quick to withdraw in the face of superior Soviet combat power."[55] In contrast, the JCS observed, the United States has "much more experience in the difficult task of projecting power to remote, hostile areas."[56]

Some Western analysts have argued that Moscow can compensate for these assorted inadequacies by employing "proxy" (i.e., Cuban) troops for overseas interventionary operations, and by using bases in friendly countries as a substitute for aircraft carriers. Certainly Cuban forces have proven a decisive factor in Angola and Ethiopia, and Soviet supply operations in this area have clearly benefitted from the use of air and naval facilities in Libya, Ethiopia, Guinea, and South Yemen. But it is also important to recognize that there are limitations to such arrangements, and that the United States also makes use of proxy forces and overseas bases to support its interventionary operations. Before concluding our assessment of U.S. and Soviet projection forces, therefore, it is necessary to compare and evaluate these subsidiary capabilities.

Turning first to "proxy" forces, it is undeniable that the introduction of Cuban forces has radically altered the military equation in Africa. Some 36,000 Cuban troops are believed to be operating in Angola and Ethiopia, and another few thousand in Guinea, Libya, Mozambique, Zambia, and a number of other countries.[57] Conceivably, some of these forces can be shifted from one country to another in the event of future hostilities, but most experts believe that the bulk of Cuban troops remain bogged down in the continuing fighting in Angola and Ethiopia, and that Havana—given its present economic and political difficulties—cannot afford to dispatch any additional soldiers to Africa. There are clear limits, therefore, to the future availability of Cuban forces for Soviet-backed military operations in Africa and the Middle East.[58] Some analysts believe that the Russians could make use of other forces— particularly those in Libya and South Yemen—as a substitute for Cuban forces. However, the military capabilities of these countries is much more limited (Libya has only 42,000 soldiers and South Yemen has 24,000), and the leaders of both these countries have political agendas which may conflict with those of Moscow and/or which may tie up their limited military resources.

While the availability of Cuban forces has certainly enhanced Moscow's power projection capabilities in the Third World, it is essential that we also look at the allied or "proxy" forces available to Washington. Both France and Great Britain possess an extensive capability for military intervention, and both have had long experience in conducting such operations. Each of these countries also maintains two aircraft carriers in active service (assets which neither the Soviet Union nor any of its allies yet possess), along with well-equipped paratroop and counterinsurgency forces which have seen active service in Africa, Asia, and the Middle East. France, moreover, has a substancial military presence in Africa and now maintains upwards of 14,000 combat troops in the region (1,000 in the Central African Republic, 4,500 in Djibouti, 4,000 on Reunion Island, 1,500 in Senegal, and smaller amounts in several other French-speaking countries).[59] The United States can also look to other countries—including Israel, Egypt, and Morocco—as a source of "proxy" forces in future African and Middle Eastern conflicts. All three countries have volunteered to cooperate with Washington in future conflicts with their Soviet-backed neighbors, and all have sizeable, well-armed forces with considerable experience in ground combat operations.[60] The United States cannot, of course, assume that any of these countries will automatically support future U.S. interventionary operations in the region, but it is obvious that any full accounting of "proxy" forces must include these capabilities along with those of potential Soviet allies.

Looking now at the question of bases, we find a similar pattern of questionable Soviet assets. In the past few years, Moscow has made extensive use of air and port facilities in Libya, Ethiopia, Guinea, and Southern Yemen to supply its allies in Africa and the Middle East. These are not, however, Soviet military bases in the sense that they are secured by treaty and protected by Soviet forces. The U.S.S.R.'s continued access to these facilities is contingent on the continued friendly relations with the government in power—a situation that can, as demonstrated by developments in Egypt and Somalia (where bases once used by the Soviets are now being used by the United States), change

131

literally overnight. Indeed, it is entirely possible that Moscow will be denied access to some of these facilities in the event of regional hostilities (just as Washington was denied access to some of *its* facilities during the 1973 Arab-Israeli conflict), while shifting political loyalties could someday result in the loss of these bases altogether (as occurred in Egypt and Somalia). Of course, Washington may also encounter such difficulties when attempting to use its new basing facilities in Egypt, Oman, Kenya, and Somalia, but it nevertheless retains an overall advantage because its bases at Diego Garcia (in the Indian Ocean), at Subic Bay (in the Philippines) and on Okinawa are secured by treaty and protected by U.S. forces. In many likely contingencies, moreover, Washington can count on access to U.S. or allied bases in Western Europe, Australia, and the Mediterranean.[61]

Conclusion

When all of these factors are weighed and measured, it is obvious that the United States maintains a far more formidable capacity for long-distance interventionary operations than that possessed by the Soviet Union. As noted by the RAND Corporation in a major 1977 assessment of Soviet and American projection forces, "gross Soviet capabilities" for overseas intervention "do not remotely equal the gross capabilities the United States could potentially bring to bear." Although this finding has had to be modified slightly by recent additions to the Soviet fleet (particularly the appearance of the *Kiev*-class carrier and the *Ivan Rogov* assault ship), the Joint Chiefs of Staff drew the same general conclusion in its Fiscal 1982 assessment of U.S. and Soviet capabilities. Noting the continued U.S. advantage in carrier-based aviation, Marine amphibious strength, intercontinental airlift, C³ and military doctrine, the JCS affirmed that "Soviet advances notwithstanding," the United States "is generally superior to the Soviet Union in those types of combat forces that are most appropriate for rapidly projecting power to areas remote from either homeland."[62]

This does not mean, of course, that Moscow lacks a significant power projection capability. Recent events in Africa indicate that the Soviet Union is fully capable of providing its allies and clients with substantial logistical and technical support. Moscow has also developed a modest capacity for long-range intervention against unsophisticated or disorganized opponents within reach of Soviet or allied bases. Unlike the United States, however, the U.S.S.R. does not now possess a capacity for full-scale military intervention against a determined or well-equipped adversary located any distance from Soviet territory. One cannot conclude from this that Moscow will not therefore engage in such operations—but it does suggest that Soviet leaders would have to face such a decision with far more caution—and fear of failure—than their American counterparts.

FOOTNOTES
TO APPENDIX

1. U.S. Congress, Congressional Budget Office, *U.S. Projection Forces: Requirements, Scenarios, and Options* (Washington, D.C.: author, 1978), p. 3. (Hereinafter cited as: CBO, *Projection Forces.*)

2. George S. Brown, *United States Military Posture for FY 1979* (Washington, D.C.: Department of Defense, 1978), p. 17.

3. CBO, *Projection Forces*, pp. 1-6.

4. Harold Brown, *Department of Defense Annual Report, Fiscal Year 1980* (Washington, D.C.: Department of Defense, 1979), pp. 30-1.

5. Harold Brown, *Department of Defense Annual Report, Fiscal Year 1981* (Washington, D.C.: Department of Defense, 1980), p. 23.

6. Cited in *The Defense Monitor*, vol. IV, no. 7 (September, 1975), p. 5.

7. Quoted in *The New York Times*, January 24, 1980.

8. H. Brown, *DOD Annual Report FY81*, *pp. 62-3.*

9. Quoted in *The Wall Street Journal*, January 28, 1981.

10. International Institute for Strategic Studies, *The Military Balance, 1979-80* (London: author, 1979), pp. 7-8. (Hereinafter cited as: IISS, *Military Balance 79-80.*)

11. See: *The Washington Star*, December 5, 1979; and *The Washington Post*, December 6, 1979. See also: David A. Quinlan, "The Marine Corps as a Rapid Deployment Force," *Marine Corps Gazette*, March 1980, pp. 32ff.

12. CBO, *Projection Forces*, pp. 9-11; IISS, *Military Balance 79-80*, p. 6. See also: *The Washington Star*, April 8, 1980; *Christian Science Monitor*, April 22, 1980.

13. On the Delta Team, see: *The New York Times*, April 28, 1980.

14. CBO, *Projection Forces*, pp. 11-12; IISS, *Military Balance 79-80*, pp. 8-9. For data on payload capabilities, see also: *Jane's All the World's Aircraft, 1976-77* (New York: Franklin Watts, 1976), pp. 319-23. (Hereinafter cited as *Jane's Aircraft 76-77.*)

15. For discussion, see: John J. Stocker, "Rapid Deployment Forces," Issue Brief No. IB80027, Congressional Research Service, Library of Congress, Washington, D.C., March 24, 1980. See also: "CX Operational Date Postponed Two Years," *Aviation Week & Space Technology* (October 20, 1980), pp. 30-1.

16. CBO, *Projection Forces*, pp. 15-16.

17. *The Wall Street Journal*, March 5, 1981. See also: "Reagan Sets A Course to Reinforce the Navy," *Business Week* (December 8, 1980), p. 31.

18. D.C. Jones, *Military Posture FY82*, p. 85.

19. *Ibid.*

20. Clarence A. Robinson, Jr., "Rapid Deployment Force Buildup Likely," *Aviation Week & Space Technology* (February 16, 1981), p. 86.

21. IISS, *Military Balance 79-80*, p. 7; Norman Polmar, *The Ships and Aircraft of the U.S. Fleet*, 11th Ed. (Annapolis: U.S. Naval Institute, 1978), pp. 122-43.

22. *The Wall Street Journal*, March 5, 1981; OJCS, *Military Posture FY82*, pp. 51-2.

23. Based on estimates provided to the author by Randall Forsberg of the Institute for Defense and Disarmament Studies, Brookline, Mass.

24. Quoted in *The New York Times*, March 5, 1981.

25. *The Wall Street Journal*, March 5, 1981.

26. IISS, *Military Balance 79-80*, pp. 5-11.

27. See: Peter H. Vigor, "The Soviet View of War," and Malcolm Mackintosh, "Soviet Military Policy," in Michael MccGwire, ed., *Soviet Naval Developments* (New York: Praeger, 1973), pp. 16-30 and 57-69, respectively.

28. See: Keith A. Dunn, "Power Projection or Influence: Soviet Capabilities for the 1980s," *Naval War College Review* (September-October, 1980), pp. 32-33.

29. See: Ken Booth, "Military Power, Military Force, and Soviet Foreign Policy," in MccGwire, *Soviet Naval Developments*, pp. 31-66.

30. See: James M. McConnell and Bradford Dismukes, "Soviet Diplomacy of Force in the Third World," *Problems of Communism* (January February, 1979), pp. 14-27. .

31. *The New York Times*, February 1, 1980.

32. See: Christopher D. Jones, "Just Wars and Limited Wars," *World Politics* (October, 1975), pp. 44-68.

33. Graham H. Turbinville, "Warsaw Pact Amphib Ops in Northern Europe," *Marine Corps Gazette* (October, 1976), pp. 20-7.

34. Dunn, "Power Projection or Influence," pp. 39-40.

35. Michael MccGwire, "Parallel Naval Developments," in MccGwire, *Soviet Naval Developments*, p. 165.

36. Graham Turbiville, "Soviet Airborne Forces," *Army* (April, 1976), pp. 18-27.

37. D.C. Jones, *Military Posture FY82*, pp. 47-8.

38. IISS, *Military Balance 79-80*, p. 11. See also: "USSR's Airlift About One-Fourth of U.S.," *Armed Forces Journal* (April, 1980), pp. 17, 63; and, William Schneider, "Soviet Military Airlift," *Air Force* (March, 1980), pp. 80-86.

39. Siegfried Breyer and Norman Polmar, *Guide to the Soviet Navy*, 2nd ed. (Annapolis: U.S. Naval Institute, 1977), pp. 112-17. See also: *Jane's Fighting Ships*.

40. See: Gary Charbonneau, "The Soviet Navy and Forward Deployment," *U.S. Naval Institute Proceedings* (March, 1979), pp. 35-40.

41. See: Michael MccGwire, "The Rationale for the Development of Soviet Seapower," *U.S. Naval Institute Proceedings* (May, 1980), pp. 155-83.

42. IISS, *Military Balance 79-80*, p. 11. See also: Robert P. Berman, *Soviet Air Power in Transition* (Washington, D.C.: Brookings Institution, 1978).

43. Dunn, "Power Projection or Influence," p. 33.

44. *Ibid.*, pp. 33-5.

45. H. Brown, *DOD Annual Report FY80*, p. 90.

46. Breyer and Polmar, *Guide to the Soviet Navy*, pp. 298-306; *Jane's Fighting Ships 1976-77*, pp. 726-7.

47. *Aerospace Daily* (October 17, 1978), p. 219.

48. Breyer and Polmar, *Guide to the Soviet Navy*, p. 493.

49. D.C. Jones, *Military Posture FY82*, p. 47.

50. See: Dunn, "Power Projection or Influence," pp. 35-7.

51. *Ibid.*, p. 36.

52. D.C. Jones, *Military Posture FY82*, pp. 46-8.

53. *Ibid.*, p. 47.

54. Dunn, "Power Projection or Influence," pp. 38-9

55. D.C. Jones, *Military Posture FY82*, p. 51.

56. *Ibid.*, p. 46.

57. Volman, A Continent Besiged, pp. 26-7.

58. For discussion, see: Volman, *A Continent Besieged*, pp. 6-8, 14-15.

59. *Ibid.*, pp. 9-12. pp. 8-9, 26-27.

60. *Ibid.*, pp. 9-12.

61. For discussion see: Dunn, "Power Projection or Influence," pp. 40-3.

62. D.C. Jones, *Military Posture FY82*, pp. 47-8.

IPS PUBLICATIONS

Research Guide to Current
Military and Strategic Affairs
William M. Arkin

The first comprehensive guide to public information sources on the U.S. military establishment. Soviet and other foreign military affairs, and global strategic issues. Provides descriptions of all basic research tools. Topics include: the U.S. military defense policy and posture; the defense budget; arms sales and military aid; weapons systems; NATO arms control and disarmament; and intelligence operations. Indispensable for anyone interested in current military and strategic affairs. $15.95 (paper, $7.95).

Real Security: Restoring American
Power in a Dangerous Decade
Richard J. Barnet

"*Real Security* is a *tour de force*, a gift to the country. One of the most impassioned and effective arguments for sanity. and survival that I have ever read." —Dr. Robert L. Heilbroner

"An inspired and inspiring achievement. . . a first salvo in the campaign to turn our current security policies—diplomatic, military, and economic—in the direction of rationality. It may well be the basic statement around which opponents of unalloyed confrontation can gather. It will have great impact." —John Marshall Lee, Vice Admiral, USN (Ret.)

"As a summary of the critical literature on the arms race, Barnet's brief essay is an important antidote to hawkish despair." —*Kirkus Reviews*. $10.95. (paper, $4.95).

Dubious Specter:
A Skeptical Look at the Soviet Nuclear Threat
Fred Kaplan

Do the Soviets really threaten American ICBMs with a devastating surprise attack? Will Soviet military doctrine lead the Russians to threaten nuclear war in order to wring concessions from the West? Do Soviet leaders think they can fight and win a nuclear war? Fred Kaplan separates the myths from the realities about U.S. and Soviet nuclear stockpiles and strategies and provides the necessary background for understanding current debates on arms limitations and military costs. $4.95.

The Counterforce Syndrome: A Guide to U.S. Nuclear Weapons and Strategic Doctrine
Robert C. Aldridge

This study discloses the shift from "deterence" to "counterforce" in the U.S. strategic doctrine. A thorough, newly-revised summary and analysis of U.S. strategic nuclear weapons and military policy including descriptions of MIRVs, MARVs, Trident systems, cruise missiles, and M-X missiles in relation to the aims of a U.S. first-strike attack. $4.95.

The New Generation of Nuclear Weapons
Stephen Daggett

An updated summary of strategic weapons, including American and Soviet nuclear hardware. These precarious new technologies may provoke startling shifts in strategic policy, leading planners to consider fighting "limited nuclear wars" or developing a preemptive first strike capability. $3.00.

The Rise and Fall of the 'Soviet Threat': Domestic Sources of the Cold War Consensus
Alan Wolfe

A timely essay demonstrating that American fear of the Soviet Union tends to fluctuate according to domestic factors as well as in relation to the military and foreign policies of the USSR. Wolfe contends that recurring features of American domestic politics periodically coalesce to spur anti-Soviet sentiment, contributing to increased tensions and dangerous confrontations.

"At this moment, one could hardly want a more relevant book." —*Kirkus Reviews*. $4.95.

Supplying Repression: U.S. Support for Authoritarian Regimes Abroad
Michael T. Klare and Cynthia Arnson

A comprehensive discussion of the programs and policies through which the U.S. supports police and internal security forces in repressive Third World countires.

"Very important, fully documented indictment of U.S. role in supplying rightist Third World governments with the weaponry and know-how of repression." —*The Nation*. $9.95 (paper, $4.95.).

Soviet Policy in the Arc of Crisis
Fred Halliday

The crescent of nations extending from Ethiopia through the Arab world to Iran and Afghanistan has become the setting of an intense new geopolitical drama. In this incisive study, Halliday reviews the complex role played there by the Soviet Union—a role shaped as much by caution as by opportunity, as much by reaction to American moves as by Soviet initiative. Above all, the Soviet role is defined and limited by the indigenous politics of the region. $4.95.

Resurgent Militarism
Michael T. Klare and the Bay Area
Chapter of the Inter-University Committee

An analysis of the origins and consequences of the growing militaristic fevor which is spreading from Washington across the nation. The study examines America's changing strategic position since Vietnam and the political and economic forces which underlie the new upsurge in militarism. $2.00.

Beyond the "Vietnam Syndrome":
U.S. Interventionism in the 1980s
Michael T. Klare

A study of the emergence of a new U.S. interventionist military policy. Shows how policy makers united to combat the "Vietnam Syndrome"—the public's resistance to American military involvement in future Third World conflicts—and to relegitimate the use of military force as an instrument of foreign policy. Includes a close look at the Pentagon's "Rapid Deployment Force," and a study of comparative U.S. Soviet transcontinental intervention capabilities. $4.95.

The Lean Years:
Politics in the Age of Scarcity
Richard J. Barnet

A lucid and startling analysis of basic global resources: energy, non-fuel minerals, food, water, and human labor. The depletion and maldistribution of supplies bodes a new global economic, political and military order in the 1980s.

"... brilliantly informed book ... cogent, aphoristic pulling-together of the skeins of catastrophic scarcity in 'the coming postpetroleum world ..."—*Publishers Weekly.* $12.95.

After the Shah
Fred Halliday

Important background information on the National Front, the Tudeh Party, the religious opposition and many other groups whose policies and programs will determine Iran's future. $2.00.

Feeding the Few:
Corporate Control of Food
Susan George

The author of *How the Other Half Dies* has extended her critique of the world food system which is geared towards profit not people. This study draws the links between the hungry at home and those abroad, exposing the economic and political forces pushing us towards a unified global food system. $4.95.

Global Reach:
The Power of the Multinational Corporations
Richard Barnet and Roland Müller

"A searching, provocative inquiry into global corporations... Barnet and Müller are trenchant and telling in their discussion of the possible end of the nation-state, and have some penetrating views on 'economic imperialism' and future changes in employment patterns and the standard of living under the domination of the global oligopolists." —*Publishers Weekly*. $7.95.

The Crisis of the Corporation
Richard Barnet

Now a classic, this essay analyzes the power of the multinational corporations which dominate the U.S. economy, showing how the growth of multinationals inevitably results in an extreme concentration of economic and political power in a few hands. The result, according to Barnet, is a cirsis for democracy itself. $1.50.

Decoding Corporate Camouflage:
U.S. Business Support for Apartheid
Elizabeth Schmidt
Foreword by Congressman Ronald Dellums

By exposing the decisive role of U.S corporations in sustaining apartheid, this study places highly-touted employment "reforms" in the context of the systematic economic exploitation and political repression of the black South African majority.

"... forcefully presented." —*Kirkus Revies.* $4.95.

South Africa:
Foreign Investment and Apartheid
Lawrence Litvak, Robert DeGrasse, and Kathleen McTigue

A critical examiniation of the argument that multinationals and foreign investment operate as a force for progressive change in South Africa. "Its concise and well-documented debunking of the myth that foreign investment will eventually change the system of exploitation and repression in South Africa deserves wide reader-ship ... Highly recommended." —*Library Journal.* $3.95.

A Continent Besieged:
Foreign Military Activities in Africa Since 1975
Daniel Volman

A study of the growing military involvement of the two super-powers and their allies in Africa. $2.00.

The Nicaraguan Revolution:
A Personal Report
Richard R. Fagen

Tracing the history of the Nicaraguan Revolution, Fagen focuses on six legacies that define current Nicaraguan reality: armed struggle; internationalization of the conflict; national unity; demo-cratic visions; death, destruction and debts; and political bank-ruptcy. This primer on the state of Nicaraguan politics and economics provides an insightful view of the Sandinist quest for power and hegemony. The report contains twenty photographs by Marcelo Montecino and appendices with the basic documents necessary for understanding contemporary Nicaraguan affairs. $4.00.

Chile: Economic 'Freedom'
and Political Repression
Orlando Letelier

A trenchant analysis by the former leading official of the Allende government who was assassinated by the Pinochet junta. This essay demonstrates the necessary relationship between an economic development model which benefits only the wealthy few and the political terror which has reigned in Chile since the overthrow of the Allende regime. $1.00.

Assassination on Embassy Row
John Dinges and Saul Landau

A devastating political document that probes all aspects of the Letelier-Moffitt assassinations, interweaving the investigations of the murder by the FBI and the Institute.

"...An engrossing study of international politics and subversion..." —*Kirkus Reviews.* $14.95.

Human Rights and Vital Needs
Peter Weiss

Delivered one year after the assassination of Orlando Letelier and Ronni Karpen Moffitt, this extraordinary address commemorates them by calling for a human rights policy that includes not only political and civil rights, but economic, social, and cultural rights as well. $1.00.

The Federal Budget
and Social Reconstruction
Marcus Raskin, Editor

This study describes the Federal Budget, sets new priorities for government spending and presents alternative policies for defense, energy, health and taxation.

"The issuance of this report is a major political event and a challenge to mainstream ideology. It should be widely purchased." —*Library Journal.* $8.95.

Postage and Handling:
All orders must be prepaid. For delivery within the USA, please add 15% of order total. For delivery outside the USA, add 20%. Standard discounts available upon request.

Please write the Institute for Policy Studies, 1901 Que Street, N.W., Washington, D.C. 20009 for our complete catalog of publications and films.